"[The visual arts] were formerly the private property of sovereigns, and were confined to what may be called the luxuries of art....The museums of to-day open their doors to all the world, and the scope of their collections has broadened to meet the public needs."

MARTIN BRIMMER, *American Architect and Building News*, October 30, 1880.

"Generosity is contagious. Here it will always have its reward; and thus the chief reliance of the friends of the Museum for its future lies in the hope of the good-will of all, the willing gifts of the wealthy, and that popular support which its friends mean to make it deserve."

THOMAS GOLD APPLETON
The Museum of the Fine Arts:
A Companion to the Catalogue
(Boston, 1877), pp. 75-76.

"...in offering this collection to the people through the Museum of Fine Arts my wife and I are not making 'noble gestures'....We are not 'Patrons of Art' or 'Public Benefactors'....We accept with pleasure only one label: 'Useful Citizens.'"

MAXIM KAROLIK, December 10, 1949 ("A Letter to the Director," quoted in *M. and M. Karolik Collection of American Paintings, 1815-1865*, Cambridge, Mass., 1949, p. xiv.)

THE GREAT BOSTON COLLECTORS:

Paintings from the Museum of Fine Arts

by Carol Troyen and Pamela S. Tabbaa

Distributed by
Northeastern University Press

Museum of Fine Arts
Boston

The exhibition and catalogue are made possible by a grant from New England Mutual Life Insurance Company on the occasion of its 150th anniversary.

Copyright © 1984 by
Museum of Fine Arts, Boston,
Massachusetts
ISBN: 0-87846-247-3
Library of Congress Catalogue Card
Number: 84-62729
Typeset and printed by Acme Printing
Company, Medford, Massachusetts
Most of the photographic work for the
catalogue was done by John C. Lutsch, Alan
B. Newman, and John D. Woolf of the
Department of Photographic Services.
Designed by Carl Zahn

Frontispiece:
Music room, Robert Dawson Evans House,
17 Gloucester Street, Boston, ca. 1910,
showing portrait by Sir Joshua Reynolds
and, reflected in the mirror, Vigée-LeBrun's
Portrait of a Young Woman (no. 25).

Foreword

The Museum of Fine Arts is honored that the New England Mutual Life Insurance Company has chosen to celebrate its 150th anniversary by sponsoring "The Great Boston Collectors" exhibition and catalogue. The project salutes a group of public-spirited Bostonians whose gifts form the core of the Museum's paintings collection. It coincides with a major renovation of the paintings galleries; thus, New England Mutual Life's sponsorship of the exhibition enables the public to view a large group of the Museum's most admired and important paintings, which would otherwise be inaccessible.

On behalf of the trustees, overseers, and staff of the Museum of Fine Arts, I extend our deep gratitude for the vision and civic leadership New England Life has demonstrated by this support.

RICHARD D. HILL
President, Museum of Fine Arts, Boston

It is a privilege for New England Life to sponsor "The Great Boston Collectors" exhibition on the occasion of our 150th Anniversary. As a national company headquartered in Boston, we feel it most appropriate to salute these eminent Boston men and women who so generously contributed to the Museum's fine collection. That this remarkable collection is available to enjoy is a valuable reminder of the importance of philanthropy in the arts and of the contributions individuals and corporations have made over the years to the quality of life in our city. Being part of this heritage makes "The Great Boston Collectors" a particularly significant part of our 150th anniversary celebration.

EDWARD E. PHILLIPS
Chairman, New England Life

Contents

In February of 1915, the Robert Dawson Evans Memorial Paintings Wing opened to the public, accompanied by an exhibition of some one hundred paintings lent by local collectors. Seventy years later, as we prepare for the reopening of the newly refurbished and climate-controlled Evans Wing, we offer a reprise of that exhibition, saluting many of the same generous Bostonians and their spiritual descendants, the succeeding generations of great Boston collectors. The lenders to the 1915 exhibition are among those whom we now consider to have been our greatest benefactors, and the art they most admired still forms the cornerstone of the paintings collection. These turn-of-the-century Bostonians preferred the work of local painters, such as Copley, Allston, and Sargent, and that of French artists of the Barbizon and Impressionist schools. And (with the addition of nineteenth-century American paintings, acquired for the Museum by Maxim Karolik) these are the great strengths of the paintings collection today.

From the founding of the Museum in 1870 through the opening of the Evans Wing and continuing to the present, Boston's great collectors have been passionate champions of particular schools and styles, rather than encyclopedic accumulators. They have been seekers of knowledge as well as beauty – explorers of new fields. Most were self-taught, often learning from the artists whose work they later bought. Their collections were deep, rather than broad. Thus, the Museum now owns over fifty paintings by Copley, some 150 works by Millet, thirty-nine by Monet – strengths no other Museum can duplicate, and strengths that directly reflect the enthusiasms of Boston's collectors. More than any other institution's, the paintings collection of the Museum of Fine Arts is a living history of Boston's taste.

Although the Museum has organized many exhibitions honoring individual collectors, this is the first to celebrate the taste of the patrons of the past, through whose collective generosity the paintings collection of the Museum of Fine Arts has achieved its current stature. Unlike the great public collections of New York (built around the Havemeyer and Lehman bequests) and Chicago (where the leading names are Ryerson and Palmer), few individual personalities predominate in Boston. Rather, there have been a host of good collectors and donors whose special insights and singular taste have shaped the Museum. Their temperaments have varied greatly, from the shy, retiring Martin Brimmer (the Museum's first president) to the exuberant Thomas Gold Appleton (its first published critic) but they have been united in their astuteness and their devotion to this institution; they built their collections with a concern for Boston's needs. Dr. Denman Waldo Ross, whose striking Monet *Cliffs of the Petites Dalles* was the first painting by that master to enter the Museum's collection, had wide-ranging interests that eventually benefited every department of the Museum. John Taylor Spaulding, the donor of an unsurpassed collection of Japanese prints, subsequently gave a group of Impressionist, Post-Impressionist, and early twentieth-century century American paintings designed to complement the Museum's holdings in these areas. And the flamboyant Maxim Karolik worked in partnership with the Museum to build a collection of nineteenth-century American art, resulting in a gift of over 300 works, by far the largest group of paintings presented to the Museum by any single benefactor. It transformed the Museum's strong representation of local artists into what is arguably the most comprehensive collection of American art in the nation. These and the other great collectors celebrated in this exhibition – Henry Lee Higginson, the Warrens, Robert Treat Paine, 2nd, the Edwards family – sought to share with the people of Boston objects of great beauty, objects meant to inspire and educate. This exhibition demonstrates the rich and rewarding fruits of their labors.

A further testimony to the foresight of these great Boston collectors is the number of exhibitions drawn primarily from the permanent collection of the Museum. Within the last ten years, we have organized exhibitions saluting those collectors' traditional favorites: John Singleton Copley (1976 and 1980), Claude Monet (1977), William Morris Hunt (1979), Washington Allston (1979), and most recently, Jean-François Millet (1984), whose works from the Museum's collection are now on view in Japan. The heritage of American art in this city was studied in the traveling exhibition "The Boston Tradition" (1980), and the dedication of Boston collectors to French art was a leitmotif in the exhibition "Corot to Braque" (1979), shown in Japan and in five American cities. It is fitting that the current exhibition, which brings together the best paintings presented to the Museum by its esteemed benefectors, is shown here in Boston as a prelude to the opening of the renovated galleries of the Evans Wing.

This exhibition was organized, and its catalogue written, by Carol Troyen, Associate Curator of American Paintings, and Pamela Tabbaa, of European Paintings. Their research acquaints us all with an important chapter in the history of the Museum and of the tastes and interests of our predecessors; at the same time, it presents our distinguished permanent collection of paintings in a new context. The project was developed under the direction of Theodore E. Stebbins, Jr., John Moors Cabot Curator of American Paintings, with many contributions by other members of the staff of the Department of Paintings.

Finally, we at the Museum of Fine Arts are deeply grateful to New England Mutual Life Insurance Company, which as part of its 150th Anniversary has honored the Museum with a major grant toward the preparation of the exhibition and catalogue. Their grant is the first contribution of such magnitude by a local corporation specifically for an exhibition project; thus, their endorsement of an enterprise saluting great Bostonians of the past is especially fitting. Without their support "The Great Boston Collectors" would not have been possible.

Jan Fontein

Acknowledgments

The kind of community spirit shown by the great Boston collectors we salute in this exhibition has been reflected in the Museum by our many colleagues on the staff, who have given generously of their time, their expertise, and their support to ensure its success. We have benefited greatly from their cooperation and have been buoyed by the sense of community the exhibition has generated.

Our first thanks go to the Director, Jan Fontein, who urged us to celebrate the permanent collection of paintings in a special exhibition, and whose initial enthusiasm for an exhibition honoring the builders of that collection encouraged us to pursue the project. We are most grateful for his support and for the hours he dedicated to discussions of the great Boston collectors. Equally generous with time and counsel has been Theodore E. Stebbins, Jr., the John Moors Cabot Curator of American Paintings, who served as adviser to the project and who with great patience helped to shape the selection of works.

Many members of the Paintings Department have given time and energy to this exhibition, and we are very much in their debt. Trevor Fairbrother, Assistant Curator of American Paintings, made many helpful recommendations about the concept and contents of the exhibition, and Cynthia Schneider and Alexandra Murphy, both Assistant Curators of European Paintings, contributed useful ideas during the initial planning stages. Patricia Loiko's common-sense approach to the exhibition's numerous logistical problems saved us much time and energy.

An exhibition drawn entirely from one museum's permanent collection places extraordinary demands on its conservation staff, and we wish to express our deepest thanks to Alain Goldrach, Conservator of Paintings, and to Brigitte Smith, Jean Woodward, and Irene Konefal for the many hours they dedicated to preparing the paintings for exhibition. The fruits of their skillful and sensitive efforts will be seen in the galleries long after this show closes. The work they have done on the Pannini, the Sargent, and the Courbet (to mention only a few) has deepened our understanding of the great beauty of these masterworks, and their recognition of the subtle quality of such paintings as the Cropsey has drawn our attention to their merit. We are equally grateful to James Barter, Conservation Assistant, for his careful attention to the paintings' frames.

The production of the catalogue for "The Great Boston Collectors" required the cooperation of many dedicated hands. Erica Hirshler assisted us in our research for the catalogue and cheerfully assumed the tedious and time-consuming task of preparing the captions. The many drafts of the catalogue were typed by Mark Palmer with characteristic good humor. Especially helpful has been Nancy Allen and her gracious staff in the Library; under their guidance the authors were able to discover many fascinating events in the Museum's history. Gathering the illustrations for the essays that follow caused us to make great demands on both the Library and Photographic Services Department, demands that were unfailingly met with efficiency and great courtesy.

The monumental task of photographing virtually every painting in the exhibition was organized by Janice Sorkow, Manager of Photographic Services, and carried out by Alan Newman and his staff. This enormous undertaking could not have succeeded without the almost daily assistance of Jack Morrison, Cliff Theriault, and the Buildings and Grounds Staff.

We would also like to thank the members of the Department of Publications, whose enthusiasm for the paintings collection and its history is reflected in this book. Carl Zahn, Director of Publications, has produced a book that is as handsome as it is clear and readable. Judy Spear's diligent editing has greatly improved the text.

The elegant installation of the exhibition was planned by Judith Downes and Tom Wong of the Design department; we are extremely grateful for their advice and encouragement from the beginning of the project. Laboring behind the scenes at all stages of the exhibition have been Kathy Duane, Exhibitions Project Manager, and George Peabody Gardner III, Assistant to the Director; their efforts to coordinate the many hands involved in "The Great Boston Collectors" is greatly appreciated.

CAROL TROYEN
PAMELA S. TABBAA

Fig. 1
Museum of Fine Arts in Copley Square, ca. 1900.

In the amusement column of the *Boston Daily Globe* of July 4, 1876, positioned between an advertisement for Black's new dissolving Stereopticon entertainment and an invitation to view David Neal's "magnificent" painting *The First Meeting of Mary Stuart and Rizzio* at the Brainard Art Gallery (admission 25¢) was a discreet announcement:

> THE MUSEUM OF FINE ARTS
> will be opened to the Public on
> Tuesday, July 4,
> in the NEW BUILDING at the corner of
> Dartmouth Street and Huntington Avenue.
> The Museum will be open daily from
> 10 A.M. until 6 P.M.
> Admission 25 cents;
> free admission on Saturdays.

Two days later, in the July 6 *Daily Globe*, the Museum of Fine Arts announced an exhibition of old master paintings from the gallery of the Duke of Montpensier, as well as French, Dutch, and American paintings, "antiquities from Egypt, Cyprus and Greece, a gallery of casts from the best sculptures; collections of porcelain, glass, carved wood, tapestry, embroidery, etc." This more detailed description was designed to distinguish the new institution from other "museums" appearing in the same newspaper column – the so-called Boston Museum (actually a vaudeville theater), which was featuring The Great Hermann with his "matchless entertainment of mystery and magic," or the Boylston Museum (another variety theater) with Mlle. Zitella's female minstrels ("who in looks and form defy the efforts of the sculptor"). And so, coinciding with the fireworks, picnics, sailing regattas, and other patriotic exercises and festivities attendant to the great Centennial Fourth of July celebration of 1876, was opened Boston's first museum devoted entirely to the fine arts.

The Museum of Fine Arts had been incorporated by the Massachusetts legislature in February of 1870, the same year as the opening of the Corcoran Gallery of American Art in Washington, D. C., and the founding of the Metropolitan Museum in New York City. For the first six years of its existence, it occupied the third-floor galleries of the Boston Athenaeum on Beacon Street. In fact, it was the severe crowding of the exhibition galleries of the Athenaeum – which since its founding as a library society in 1807 had been the main repository in Boston for "serious" paintings – that prompted such prominent Bostonians as financier Henry P. Kidder, merchant and amateur painter Charles C. Perkins, the philanthropist Martin Brimmer, Harvard president Charles W. Eliot, and other champions of the fine arts to form a new institution for the public display of paintings and other works of art.

The Athenaeum's history as a collector and exhibitor of paintings and sculpture lay the foundation for the activities of the Museum of Fine Arts. Over a period of nearly fifty years it had accumulated both American and European old master paintings, parallel interests established in 1828 by the first two purchases of the Fine Arts Committee: a self-portrait attributed to the great seventeenth-century Bolognese painter Annibale Carracci, and the imposing *Pat Lyon at the Forge* (no. 21) by the Boston-born painter John Neagle. And beginning in 1827, the Athenaeum also sponsored exhibitions in these areas with works culled from local collections and later from other American and European cities. Exhibitions of contemporary artists were also regularly scheduled. The Athenaeum's efforts were carried on by the Museum's founders, and the institution's very first acquisitions – coming to the Museum before the Copley Square building was even opened – were two spectacular old-master paintings, Boucher's *Halt at the Spring* and *Returning from Market* (no. 15), and *Elijah in the Desert* (no. 26), a historic work by Boston's most beloved local artist, Washington Allston. The Museum's exhibition program in its early years also followed the pattern established by the Athenaeum. The inaugural exhibition of old master paintings (the Duke of Montpensier collection, mentioned above) was followed by exhibitions of such local favorites as Allston, William Rimmer, and William Morris Hunt.

The founders saw their Museum as more than simply relieving the overtaxed Athenaeum of its burden of the public display of pictures. They believed that art could be uplifting and edifying, and wanted to contribute to the city's welfare by making it available to a broader public. They also wanted to raise the level of taste and artistic knowledge in Boston by showing works of superior quality and unquestioned authenticity. Before the Museum's founding, the interested Bostonian had limited opportunities to see genuine original works of art. Until the end of the Civil War, very few Bostonians traveled abroad and fewer still visited the great museums of Europe. And at home, paintings of quality were only sporadically shown. Ethan Allen Greenwood's New England Museum, which in 1825 had absorbed the Columbian Museum on State Street, combined the functions of both an art museum and a museum of natural history and exotica. Touring paintings, first by American artists and subsequently both old masters and contemporary European artists, could be seen in places like Faneuil Hall on the waterfront by those willing – and able – to pay the not inconsiderable 25¢ viewing fee. And there were social clubs that periodically exhibited works of art. The Boston Artists' Association – established in 1842 by such local artists as Washington Allston, Henry Sargent, and Chester Harding – sponsored exhibitions of European as well as contemporary American paintings. It was succeeded in 1855 by the Boston Art Club, which held annual exhibitions of contemporary art. The short-lived Allston Club (1866-1867) was organized by and for local artists (especially those interested in French nineteenth-century art), and its two exhibitions served as a challenge to those of the more established Athenaeum and Boston Art Club. These organizations generated pride in and patronage of local painters, but they were less successful in educating Bostonians about old master paintings.

Even after mid-century Bostonians harbored suspicions and insecurities about older European paintings, perhaps held over from the early days of the Republic, when European art was associated with monarchy and aristocratic privilege. At the same time, the budding collectors among them were easy prey for unscrupulous or ill-informed dealers who imported from Europe overattributed and even forged works, for they had little opportunity to study paintings of genuine quality. Thus, when the Museum opened its doors in 1876, many of the local collections were composed of a large number of contemporary copies of famous paintings – for a good copy of a Raphael or a Titian had the same inspirational quality as the original at the Louvre, it was believed, and was at least clearly what it seemed to be. Other collections, even when assembled by Bostonians as well educated and well traveled as Senator Charles Sumner, consisted largely of fakes, falsely attributed and overglamorized European paintings. Sumner gave his sizable collection – primarily of Dutch and Flemish paintings – to the Museum in 1874. Resolute in their determination to raise the standards of connoisseurship in Boston, the Museum's leadership ordered most of the collection sold rather than display works of inferior quality and questionable authenticity; with the money realized from the Sumner sale, the Museum bought plaster casts of famous classical statues for the benefit of art students who were among the young Museum's most enthusiastic visitors.

Designed by John H. Sturgis in a flamboyant Italian Gothic style, the new building on Copley Square at first housed paintings in two locations – the Upper Hall and the second-floor skylit Picture Gallery. When an addition, included in the original design, was completed in 1879, paintings were shown in two rooms in addition to the Upper Hall: the Picture Gallery to the left of the staircase (housing works of Vivarini, Bassano, Greuze [no. 23], Courbet [no. 33], Millet, Hunt, and Whistler) and the Allston Room (where pictures by Allston, Stuart [no. 18], Copley [no. 19], Rubens, Cuyp, Reynolds, and Turner [no. 27] were displayed). Although occupying a new building, the paintings galleries of the new museum did not at first differ radically from the third-floor rooms of the Athenaeum. Old favorites from the Athenaeum's own collections filled the walls, including Allston's *Belshazzar's Feast*, Pannini's *Picture Gallery with Views of Modern Rome* (no. 17), Ruisdael's *Landscape with a Church*, Giordano's *Golden Age*, Stuart's portraits of George Washington and Martha Washington, and Greuze's *White Hat* (no. 23), many of which have since entered the Museum's permanent collection. In addition, one could see other paintings by Stuart and Copley as well as the paintings belonging to the Duke of Montpensier that had been shown at the Athenaeum in 1874.

The duke's collection, on loan from Seville, gave Boston an opportunity to see genuine examples of works by well-known artists like Zurbarán, Murillo, and Velázquez, as well as the lesser-known Valdes Leal, Herrera, and Morales. While the Museum did not acquire a major Spanish painting until 1901 (no. 6), early exposure to works of high quality undoubtedly sparked Boston's interest in that area.

The institution that opened to the public on July 4, 1876, at the corner of Dartmouth Street and Huntington Avenue, was conceived not solely as a paintings collection, however, but rather as a general art museum that could bring together Boston's holdings in a wide variety of fields. Several institutions in the Boston area were in need of space to exhibit their collections and, in the 1870s, transferred important parts of their holdings to the MFA. In addition to the paintings mentioned above, the Athenaeum deposited several pieces of sculpture, including Thomas Crawford's *Orpheus* (now owned by the Museum of Fine Arts), and intended to exhibit the important collection of medieval arms and armor donated to it by Colonel T. Bigelow Lawrence, which was destroyed in the great fire of 1872. Harvard University sent its collection of over 30,000 European prints left by Francis Calley Gray, and M.I.T. its collection of architectural casts. Also exhibited in the new museum were a varied group of objects, most of them lent by a variety of Boston donors (for example, G. W. Wales, C. C. Perkins, and H. P. Kidder), including Greek vases, plaster casts of classical and Renaissance sculpture; a collection of Italian Renaissance textiles, wood carvings, and metalwork (purchased by the Athenaeum with insurance funds from the destroyed Lawrence collection); Egyptian sculpture (both the famed Way collection and pieces donated by the family of John Lowell); and European decorative arts (including late eighteenth-century wall panels from the Hôtel de Montmorency in Paris, designed by Claude-Nicolas Ledoux). Interestingly, Asiatic art, whose rapid expansion later in the century was a major factor for the Museum's eventual relocation to Huntington Avenue, was represented in these early years only by a small group of Chinese and Japanese bronzes and ceramics, which were exhibited in the Loan Room with examples of European decorative arts and textiles.

The Museum by-laws of 1870 clearly state the three goals of the new institution: to make local collections available to the public, to become a "representative museum of fine arts in all their branches" (helped by the generosity of these same local collectors), and to provide instruction in the fine arts. These goals were met in the field of paintings with great enthusiasm, and with an almost immediately recognizable focus in three major areas – nineteenth-century French painting, European old master paintings, and works by local artists, both colonial and contemporary. The emphasis on collecting genuine works, and on the Museum's special responsibility to local art, was reiterated by Martin Brimmer, the Museum's first president, in an article published ten years after the institution was incorporated:

> ...no opportunity should be neglected to procure for our museums works of...original and permanent value. The fact that such works of the older painters and sculptors are daily becoming more rare and costly, as they are gradually being gathered into public collections of Europe, should be rather a stimulus than a discouragement; for at the rate at which they are now being absorbed, they will, in another generation, be almost unattainable... our Museum, too, has its local duty to perform in gathering together adequate examples of the artists associated with this neighborhood.... A Boston collection would be singularly deficient if it did not contain a full representation of Copley and Stuart, of Allston and Crawford, of Hunt and Rimmer. (*American Architect and Building News*, October 30, 1880)

American Paintings

American painting became an important part of the Museum's early history, although Bostonians' interest in these years was almost exclusively parochial: exhibitions of paintings by artists connected with Boston dominated the Museum's calendar until the early 1890s. These included a survey of contemporary American art in 1880, with special emphasis on such local painters as J. Appleton Brown, Ernest Longfellow, and J. Foxcroft Cole, and in 1882 an exhibition called "Portraits of Washington," featuring Gilbert Stuart's work. Beginning in 1879 with the

Museum's first "blockbuster," "An Exhibition of the Works of William Morris Hunt," there was a series of major exhibitions commemorating local painters: William Rimmer (1879), Gilbert Stuart (1880), Washington Allston (1881), and George Fuller (1884). To perpetuate the city's distinguished artistic tradition, the Museum's founders established in 1877 an art school (then called the School of Drawing and Painting) under the guidance of Hunt and John La Farge. Among the members of the first faculty were the esteemed artists Thomas Dewing, William Rimmer, and Otto Grundmann; by the 1890s, when Edmund Tarbell and Frank Benson joined the faculty and forged a distinctive Boston style, the Museum School gained national prominence.

The commitment to the work of local painters in the early years is also reflected by the fact that of the first three purchases made by the Museum, two were by Bostonians – Allston's *Rising of a Thunderstorm at Sea* in 1877, and Rimmer's *Evening: Fall of Day* in 1881. Gifts by subscription, another indicator of the popularity of a style or native school, were at first confined to Barbizon paintings, but soon funds were contributed toward the purchase of American works (albeit often in a French style), including examples by George Fuller and Thomas Robinson, acquired in 1887 and 1888, respectively. Local artists and their families were often quite generous to the Museum with gifts of their own paintings as well as works from their private collections; with such gifts, William Babcock, John B. Johnston, and Sarah Wyman Whitman joined the long list of the Museum's benefactors. One of the highlights of the American painting collection and the Museum's first painting by Winslow Homer, *The Fog Warning* (no. 34), was given to the Museum in 1893 by Grenville Norcross, the artist's cousin. The majority of American paintings to enter the Museum during these early years on Copley Square were given by local patrons, few of whom considered themselves specialists in American art. Rather, they saw in their paintings echoes of a European spirit, and hung them (as did the Museum in those years) alongside their Barbizon and old master pictures.

Fig. 2
William Rimmer, *Evening: Fall of Day*, 1869, chalk, charcoal, and watercolor on canvas (Purchase, 1881).

Barbizon Paintings

Of the three areas of strength in the paintings collection that developed in the Copley Square years – nineteenth-century French, old master, and American painting – the best-loved and most enthusiastically collected works were the landscapes of the French Barbizon School. The popularity of these paintings stemmed not only from their aesthetic appeal but also from the personal connections the patrons enjoyed with their creators. Many Boston collectors were also amateur artists who, beginning in the late 1840s, either studied with or became friends of the Barbizon painters during trips to France. Furthermore, Bostonians were attracted to the moral element they discerned in these paintings, and so viewed painters like Millet, with his noble images of rural laborers, as modern-day old masters. One of these collectors, Thomas Gold Appleton, wrote of Millet's paintings: "They have a Biblical severity and remind us of the gravest of the Italian masters." The taste in Boston for these modern French works dates from the 1850s, when people like William Morris Hunt (who studied with Couture and later with Jean-François Millet) and Martin Brimmer began buying Millets (see no. 31) directly from the artist. This early group of collectors also included Appleton, William Babcock (like Hunt, a student of Couture and Millet who chose to remain in Barbizon), and Edward Wheelwright, who later became a critic for *Atlantic Monthly*, a role in which he was able to reinforce Hunt's view on French painting. The key figure was William Morris Hunt, whose marriage to Louisa Perkins, daughter of a wealthy and socially prominent Boston merchant, gave him *entrée* to the city's elite social and artistic circles. He painted portraits of many eminent Bostonians in the French manner he learned abroad, and preached the merits of the Barbizon painters to his patrons. His influence affected collectors such as Quincy Adams Shaw, Henry Sayles (an Allston Club member who once owned Courbet's great painting *The Quarry* [no. 33]), Thomas Wigglesworth, Henry C. Angell, and later Susan Cornelia (Mrs. Samuel Dennis) Warren, and Robert Dawson

Fig. 3
Jean Baptiste Camille Corot, *Dante and Virgil*, ca. 1857-1859, oil on canvas (Gift of Quincy Adams Shaw, 1875).

and Maria Antoinette Evans, all of whom bought paintings by Millet, Rousseau, Daubigny, and others while their New York and Philadelphia counterparts were patronizing French academic artists. Boston's early interest in French painters can also be seen in the choice of the first two paintings bought for the Museum by public subscription: Diaz's *Path in the Forest* and Couture's *A Soldier*, a study for *The Enrollment of the Volunteers of 1792*, both given in 1877.

Old Master Paintings

The old master painting collection grew more slowly than the holdings of American and nineteenth-century French paintings, but even in the Museum's first fifteen years some exceptional works were acquired, including four of the collection's most prized eighteenth-century French paintings, the two Bouchers (see no. 15) given by the Peter Parker family in 1871, and two still lifes by Chardin – one given by Mrs. Peter Chardon Brooks in 1880 (no. 12) and the other by Martin Brimmer in 1883 (no. 13). Ironically, the most popular of the old master paintings in Boston were Italian and Netherlandish works, many of which were copies of famous masterpieces, or whose attributions have since been proved false. However, as the Museum grew, the quality of works both given and purchased improved steadily, and a greater catholicity of taste became evident. In 1889 the trustees acquired, by purchase and contribution, a group of ten paintings, most of them Dutch, that had been on loan to the Museum since 1881 from Stanton Blake. These were works with a celebrated history: they had been purchased by Blake in 1880 from the Prince Demidoff Collection at the San Donato Palace in Florence, and included Gabriel Metsu's *The Usurer*, Nicolaes Maes's *Jealous Husband*, and Jan van Huysum's exquisitely detailed *Vase of Flowers in a Niche* (no. 9). This group of paintings inaugurated a great period of old master acquisitions, received through gift and by purchase with newly available funds.

The majority of old master paintings that came to the Museum, however, were donated by private collectors – a large number of them – who are remembered for one or two major gifts. Among these many benefactors was Mrs. Frederick L. Ames, whose 1893 gift of a superb pair of Rembrandt portraits (nos. 10 and 11) filled an important gap in the Museum's Dutch paintings collection, for until that time it contained no portraits and no Rembrandts. As was the case with many of Boston's collectors, the Ameses' taste was eclectic (their collection also included Chinese jade and sixteenth- and seventeenth-century oriental carpets). Also of note were Mr. and Mrs. Henry Lee Higginson, who gave in 1893 what would become the cornerstone of the Museum's Northern Renaissance collection, the celebrated *St. Luke Painting the Virgin* by Rogier van der Weyden (no. 3). Higginson (1834-1919) is best known today as the founder of the Boston Symphony Orchestra in 1881, and indeed music, rather than paintings, was the passion of his life. His interest in the visual arts may have been sparked by his wife, Ida Agassiz, whose sister was married to the great Millet collector Quincy Adams Shaw. The Higginsons were not, however, collectors of Flemish primitives, or even specifically of old master paintings, but had a more traditional Boston collection of Barbizon pictures with a complement of contemporary American paintings, as well as copies of famous works of art. They acquired the van der Weyden at the 1889 American Art Association sale with the specific intention of giving it to the Museum.

Donations of individual masterworks were supplemented by purchases made by the Museum, purchases made possible by special acquisitions funds. In 1895 the Museum bought five old master paintings, including a Botticelli, a double portrait by the sixteenth-century North Italian painter Giovanni Battista Moroni (no. 5), a portrait by Reynolds, and Delacroix's turbulent *Lion Hunt* (no. 32). Public subscription brought another Delacroix to the Museum in that decade, the somber *Entombment*, presented in memory of Martin Brimmer, and also secured Henri Regnault's enormous *Automedon with the Horses of Achilles*. The fund drive for that picture was spearheaded by local art students in defiance of criticism of the work's vivid color and bold execution. During the same period, the Museum made some important acquisitions in fields not yet well represented in the

Fig. 4
William Morris Hunt, *Self Portrait*, 1866, oil on canvas (Purchase, William Wilkins Warren Fund, 1897).

Fig. 5
John Singer Sargent, *Portrait of Henry Lee Higginson*, 1903, oil on canvas (Harvard University Portrait Collection, Gift by Student Subscription, 1903).

collection. In 1899 the famous Turner *Slave Ship* (no. 27), which Alice Hooper had loaned to the Museum several times since its opening, was finally purchased; one of the collection's finest quattrocento paintings, Crivelli's *The Virgin with the Dead Christ and Saints Mary Magdalen and John* (no. 2), was bought in 1902 on the recommendation of the celebrated connoisseur Bernard Berenson; and in 1901 the Velázquez portrait, *Don Baltasar Carlos with a Dwarf* (no. 6), was purchased, the first major Spanish seventeenth-century painting to enter the collection and still one of the Museum's greatest masterpieces.

Boston's Artist-Advisers

The paintings purchased by the Museum in its early years were chosen by its trustees and, secondarily, by its staff, guided by General Charles G. Loring, who served the institution as trustee, curator, and then as director from 1873 until his death in 1902. Equally often, the Museum turned to locally prominent artists for guidance, and their recommendations resulted in many of the finest acquisitions of the Copley Square years. Perhaps the most influential figure was John Singer Sargent, whose status as late-nineteenth-century Boston's favorite portraitist was established at the 1888 St. Botolph Club exhibition, his first solo show in America. That exhibition marked the Boston debut of *The Daughters of Edward D. Boit* (painted in the Boit family's Paris apartment in 1882; no. 35), which quickly became one of the artist's best-known pictures and, since its presentation to the MFA by the four daughters in 1919, the American painting most strongly identified with the Museum. The popularity of Sargent's murals in the Boston Public Library (completed in 1895) resulted in his being commissioned to decorate the rotunda of the Museum's new building on Huntington Avenue, which opened in 1909. And during that period, he recommended acquisitions such as the somber portrait *Fray Hortensio Félix Paravicino* (no. 7), which Sargent called "one of the best El Greco's I ever saw."

In 1904, the year the El Greco was acquired, the Museum purchased another important Spanish picture, a portrait of Philip IV, attributed to Velázquez. Funds were supplied by Sarah Wyman Whitman, a Boston painter, pupil of William Morris Hunt, long-time friend of the Martin Brimmers, and an active supporter of the Museum of Fine Arts. In addition to the purchase fund that bears her name, Whitman gave the Museum several paintings from her personal collection, notably two landscapes by the American Impressionist John Twachtman and, exemplifying that peculiarly Boston mixture of enthusiasm for both modern and old-master paintings, urged the purchase of the magnificent gold-ground picture *The Mystical Marriage of Saint Catherine* by Barna da Siena (no. 1), which was finally acquired, again with her funds, in 1915.

Though not herself a Bostonian, Mary Cassatt was instrumental in bringing to Boston two Manets that were later given to the Museum: *Street Singer* (no. 37), bought by Sarah Choate Sears on Cassatt's advice and loaned to the Museum as early as 1905 (it entered the collection in 1966) and the powerful *Execution of the Emperor Maximilian* (no. 36). That painting was purchased in 1909 by Boston collector Frank Gair Macomber. Cassatt's letter to Macomber underscores her role as tastemaker: "I am very much interested to know that you have bought the fine Manet and delighted that our chance meeting has led to the picture going to America. It has been one of the chief interests of my life to help fine things across the Atlantic."

The Legacy of the Founders

The paintings collection in the Copley Square years was developed not by one or two or even three figures, but by a larger group of Bostonians whose interest in paintings informed their lives and benefited the Museum enormously. These people were collectors who generously gave of their time and shared their paintings with Boston, first as loans to the Museum and later as gifts. Many of these collectors were also amateur artists whose studies in Europe exposed them to a wide range of art – including contemporary French painting, which became the backbone of many of their collections. Figures such as Martin Brimmer, Thomas Gold Appleton, Quincy Adams Shaw, the Warrens, and Denman Waldo Ross typify in different ways the men and women so important to the early years of the Museum and to the life of the fine arts in Boston.

Martin Brimmer

Martin Brimmer (1829-1896), the first president of the Museum, was an ideal choice to guide the new institution for its first twenty-five years. His father, a successful merchant and mayor of Boston for two years, left Brimmer comfortable enough to be able to devote his life to public service and to indulge fully his love of literature and art. After graduation from Harvard in 1849 (and despite his always delicate health), Brimmer spent several years in France, where he studied art, returning to Boston in 1854. He served in the Massachusetts legislature for a few years and became a trustee of the Athenaeum before being appointed as first president of the Museum of Fine Arts in 1870. John Jay Chapman described him as "The best of old Boston...not quite inside the puritan tradition and ...a little sweeter by nature and less sure he was right than the true Bostonian is.... There was nothing of that austere look which comes from holding onto property and standing pat" (quoted in Edward Waldo Emerson, *The Early Years of the Saturday Club, 1855-1870*, Boston, 1918, p. 373).

Brimmer's own collection of paintings was a mix of old masters, nineteenth-century French paintings, and American works, which characterized many of the collections in Boston at the time. Among Brimmer's gifts during his lifetime were the MFA's first three Millets, a still life by Chardin (no. 13), and a triptych attributed to the Sienese painter Bartolo di Fredi. At her death his widow bequeathed an additional group of paintings to the Museum, including a sixteenth-century Italian Virgin and Child, five more Millets (among them the magnificent *Harvesters Resting* [no. 31]), a Stuart, a Hunt, two Vedders, and the elegant portrait of Mrs. Richard Skinner (no. 24) by John Singleton Copley, Boston's most celebrated portraitist and an ancestor of Mrs. Brimmer's.

Thomas Gold Appleton

Thomas Gold Appleton (1812-1884) was, like Brimmer, the son of a wealthy man who had an abiding interest in the arts. Serving as Harvard's representative on the Museum's first board of trustees, he was an unflagging supporter and helped the Museum in a number of ways. Like many of the people involved in the arts in Boston and in the early development of the Museum, Appleton was a graduate of Harvard (class of 1831) and an amateur artist. Son of Nathan Appleton, a wealthy textile manufacturer who helped found Lowell, Massachusetts, he traveled and, after 1833, lived abroad for many years, during which time he became a friend (and possibly a pupil) of the Barbizon painter Constant Troyon. In 1864 Appleton returned to Boston and settled in a house at 10 Commonwealth Avenue. He became renowned for his sharp wit, his lively essays (often on travel), his poetry, and his public spiritedness, as evidenced by his tenure as trustee of the Boston Public Library and the Boston Athenaeum and by his life-long dedication to the Museum of Fine Arts, being one of the three major contributors to the building of the Copley Square museum. Appleton was also a collector of some note – his interests included paintings, Greek vases, and Etruscan objects – and his 1884 bequest comprised several Barbizon paintings (among which were three Troyons, Rousseau's *Landscape with A Peasant Watering her Cows*, and Diaz's *Turkish Café*), as well as works by Constable, Bonington, Tintoretto, and Vedder.

In 1877 Appleton published anonymously a companion guide to the MFA in which he conducted through the Museum an imaginary friend Starbuck – "a fine fellow, one of the suburban gentlemen who live with dignity, if not much profit, on a handsome farm not many miles from Boston." In his tour of the paintings galleries "Appleton" pointed out many works on loan from the Athenaeum or the City of Boston, including those by "America's greatest painter," Washington Allston. He deplored the general lack of English paintings, while praising Reynolds's *Miss Pyne* (which, incidentally, he had given to the Museum the previous year) and the Turner *Slave Ship* (no. 27) – then on loan from Alice Hooper. He also discussed at length

Fig. 6
Martin Brimmer (1829-1896).

Fig. 7
Thomas Gold Appleton (1812-1884).

Fig. 8
Quincy Adams Shaw (1825-1908), ca. 1900.

Fig. 9
Donatello, *Madonna of the Clouds*, ca. 1425-1430, marble (Gift of Quincy Adams Shaw through Quincy A. Shaw, Jr., and Mrs. Marian Shaw Haughton, 1917).

landscape painting, particularly that of Rousseau, Millet, Corot, Troyon, and Constable, and excused his extended lecture by explaining that these works represented more than other art the taste of the time – a taste he linked with the poetry of Cowper, Wordsworth, and Byron. As for American painting, after concentrating on the Copleys, Stuarts, and Trumbulls, the author commented on living American artists, citing La Farge for his "passionate delicacy," Inness for his "breezy richness," Johnson for his "New England characterization," and Vedder for his "weird picturesqueness." Appleton deplored the lack of old master paintings and urged the buying of originals, not copies. He was also distressed that so few paintings were actually owned by the Museum and hoped "that many will get so attached to their new situation, so flattered by the excellent light and notice of thousands, that they will gladly remain."

Quincy Adams Shaw

Boston's greatest collector of Barbizon paintings, and of Millet's works in particular, was Quincy Adams Shaw (1825-1908). Shaw was a Harvard graduate (class of 1849) and son of a socially prominent and wealthy family. He made a fortune in a midwestern mining venture in the 1860s, enabling him to donate both personal

energy and financial support to philanthropic causes and community activities. Shaw was one of the first contributors to the Museum's building fund, a frequent lender to its exhibitions, and a generous donor to its collections. His interest in modern French painting may have begun during the 1850s, when he, along with other Bostonians (including Hunt and Brimmer), was in France; by the late 1860s he had amassed a large collection of Barbizon works. In 1871, he met Millet for the second time and commissioned a painting from one of the artist's sketches. Thus began what was to become the largest collection of works by Millet in the country – 56 paintings, prints, and pastels – most

of which were given to the Museum in 1917 by his heirs. Shaw's generosity to the Museum was not confined solely to works by Millet, however. In 1875, he gave Corot's large *Dante and Virgil*, the first of his Barbizon paintings to enter the collection. And over the next quarter century he contributed superb examples from his other area of great interest: painting and sculpture of the Renaissance. An altarpiece by Vivarini and an *Annunciation* by Palma Giovane came to the Museum in 1901 and a relief by Luca della Robbia in 1917; also in 1917, Shaw's heirs presented the Museum with the crown jewel of his collection: Donatello's marvelously delicate marble relief of the *Madonna of the Clouds*.

Samuel Dennis and
Susan Cornelia Warren

Although interest in Barbizon painting reached its peak in Boston during the 1860s and 1870s, local collectors eagerly accumulated such works as late as the 1890s. Samuel Dennis Warren, a successful paper manufacturer who developed Cumberland Mills (near Portland, Maine) and its surrounding village, was a trustee of the Museum from 1883 until his death in 1888. His wife, Susan Cornelia Warren, was an astute collector who, with the help of the Vose Gallery (an important force in bringing French nineteenth-century art to New England), put together one of the most important collections of Barbizon painting in the 1880s and 1890s. The Warrens' first gift to the Museum was Millet's *Young Shepherdess*, a monumental late work by Boston's favorite master and recently discovered to have been painted over one of Millet's earliest attempts at history painting. Following her husband's death, Mrs. Warren gave to the Museum a group of paintings including one each by Couture, Daubigny, and Millet, and two Corots (see no. 30) – the latter two bought directly for the Museum.

In their enthusiasm for Barbizon paintings, the Warrens were typical of Boston collectors – although the magnitude of their holdings far exceeded the norm. Characteristically Bostonian, too, was their eclecticism. Mrs. Warren was equally indefatigable as a collector of old master paintings: she owned works by Jan Brueghel, Gainsborough, Greuze, Filippino Lippi, and Dürer's teacher Wohlgemuth (whose *Death of the Virgin* was given to the Museum in Mrs. Warren's memory by her children) – and she was Isabella Stewart Gardner's chief rival for Titian's celebrated *Rape of Europa* (only Gardner's close relationship with Bernard Berenson, the agent for the picture, secured it for Fenway Court). Most of the above-mentioned paintings were included in the large "Special Exhibition of Paintings from the Collection of the late Mrs. S. D. Warren," held at the Museum in 1902, as were works by local favorites Whistler, Hunt, Inness, and La Farge.

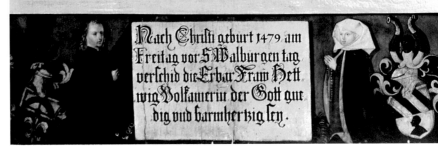

Fig. 10
Michael Wohlgemuth, *Death of the Virgin*, ca. 1479, oil on panel (Gift of the Children of Susan Cornelia Warren in memory of their mother, 1903).

Fig. 11
John Singer Sargent, *Denman Waldo Ross*, 1917, charcoal on paper (Gift of the Committee on the Museum, 1917).

Denman Waldo Ross

Brimmer, Appleton, Shaw, and the Warrens represent the first generation of great Boston collectors to dedicate their energies to the paintings collection at the MFA. Among their successors, one figure stands out in his service to the Museum: Denman Waldo Ross (1853-1935), a theorist of painting, a painter himself, and a truly remarkable collector. Graduated from Harvard in 1875, Ross continued his studies there, receiving a Ph.D. in history in 1880. He stayed at Harvard, teaching drawing and writing (the first of his books, *A Theory of Pure Design*, was published in 1907), and living until his death in his parents' large Brattle Street house in Cambridge. The extraordinary energy and astuteness with which he collected was combined with community spirit, for, beginning in 1883 and continuing to his death, Ross loaned or gave much of what he bought to the Museum of Fine Arts.

Ross traveled widely throughout Europe and the Far East, insisting on buying only the most beautiful and highest quality objects available, and excluding no country of origin, period, or medium. Thus, his brilliantly eclectic collection comprised, often in staggering quantity, Chinese porcelain, Middle Eastern textiles, Japanese paintings, European decorative arts, Persian ceramics, Egyptian mummy cloths, and of course paintings, which were in themselves a varied lot. Among his early gifts of paintings to the Museum were works from the Italian Renaissance and seventeenth-century France, a Tiepolo oil sketch (the first Tiepolo to enter the Museum), and, in 1902, the stunning portrait of William Lock (no. 28) by Thomas Lawrence, given in memory of the former director of the Museum, Charles Greely Loring. In addition, Ross's 1906 gift included the Museum's first three Monets – *Cliffs of the Petites Dalles* (no. 56), *Ravine of the Creuse*, and an early marine painting – some of which had been lent as early as 1892, showing Ross to have been on the cutting edge of taste in Boston, and a pioneer in the shift of popular taste from Barbizon to Impressionist pictures.

The Years of Transition

Despite the activity of these great patrons and the rapid growth of the paintings collection, the Museum did not have an actual Curator of Paintings until 1911. The collection was part of the Department of Western Art, and the keeper of paintings often relied on interested trustees, local collectors, and artists for advice on purchases. There were, in fact, paintings exhibitions in those years, and it is very possible that the impact of a 1910 exhibition of fifty works from New York's distinguished Frick Collection may have alerted the Museum to the need for more professional guidance for its paintings holdings. In 1911 a special fund was set up to attract to the Museum Jean Guiffrey, adjunct curator of paintings at the Louvre and a specialist in old master paintings, with a promise of $100,000 to be used for the purchase of paintings during his three-year appointment. And buy he did, his acquisitions bringing exactly the type of aristocratic, "high style" pictures the MFA had never owned. Thus entered the collection Claude's late *Apollo and the Muses on Mount Helicon* (no. 14 – a noble late work by the master), the *Portrait of a Man* by Andrea Solario, a Florentine cassone panel (the first secular work of the Italian Renaissance to enter the Museum), a Virgin and Child by Bramantino (no. 4), Guardi's *Procession of Gondolas* (no. 16), and Delaroche's portrait of the Marquis de Pastoret. With the acquisition of these works and Guiffrey's appointment, the stage was set for the Museum to dedicate a large and prominent suite of galleries to the display of paintings.

Even before Guiffrey's arrival, the collection had grown to fill eight galleries in the Copley Square building. As the numbers of paintings increased, the Museum modified its original style of exhibiting them. During the early years at Copley Square the method favored was that used at the Athenaeum of mixing country, period, and sizes of paintings in a tightly packed hanging, often with four pictures tiered to the top of the wall molding – a method of installation that found vocal detractors in the press. But by the turn of the century, the staff had begun to arrange the pictures by schools and countries, a practice that became more refined

Fig. 12
The first Picture Gallery, October 1902 (photograph by T. E. Marr) — including nos. 2, 6, 9, and
11.

with time. *The Collector* of December 1899 noted: "...cudos for coming nearest to a chronological display of paintings...," the writer then indicating that the largest drawback was now "...the absolutely neglected condition of the paintings...." The new arrangement included large paintings of varied parentage in the Upper Hall; Italian, French, and Spanish works in the First Picture Gallery immediately off the Hall; early American paintings in the Allston room; Dutch, Flemish, and German pictures in the Dutch Room; and primarily American and French cabinet pictures in the Fourth and Fifth Picture Galleries. In 1904 the press was again praising the Museum for rearranging and making less crowded the paintings galleries. No longer were paintings placed cheek to jowl and skied to the ceiling. Like paintings were hung together, either singly if very large, or double-hung with some space in between paintings – certainly not the spacious hanging favored today, but much more rational and visually less confusing than installation practices in the 1870s and 1880s.

By the 1890s the area around the Museum had become a cultural and intellectual center of Boston and one of the city's architectural showplaces. The land in front of the Museum had been reserved as a public space and proudly named Copley Square in honor of Boston's favorite colonial artist; H. H. Richardson's Trinity Church, which housed the rousing sermons of Phillips Brooks, dominated the Square since the mid-1870s, and the Boston Public Library was begun on the Boylston Street corner in 1888. And so it was, first with disbelief and then dismay, that Bostonians learned in the winter of 1899-1900 that the Museum was planning to relocate. The reasons for the move – overcrowding, possible encroachment of tall buildings, problems of light and fear of fire – though valid, did not mollify the public. Wrote one: "These are the funeral days at the Art Museum...the curtain will be rung down on a building that has not died of old age, but of diseases common to modern progress – crowding and shortsightedness.... It is almost impossible to be a landmark in this ambitious town" (*Boston Herald*, May 1, 1909). Public regret was outweighed by the enthusiastic support of trustees and major museum benefactors, and after nearly a decade of discussion the Museum of Fine Arts moved from Copley Square to the Fenway, former site of the circus and wild west shows.

In the *Boston Herald* of April 17, 1909, appeared an article beginning in part, "...It looks more and more lonesome every day for the old art museum building.... Emptiness and neglect sit upon the terracotta walls.... It will take time to find the new MFA 'way up Huntington Avenue.'" The paintings galleries were the last to close. On Sunday May 2, 1909, the last day, the Museum was open free of charge and nearly 3,000 visitors came to say farewell to a building, to favorite paintings, to an institution that had been part of Boston for thirty-three years. The building itself was razed the next year to make way for the Copley Plaza Hotel, which still occupies that prominent site. But the Museum had become overcrowded and its departments, including paintings, had grown enormously. What was in 1880 a group of just over sixty paintings grew dramatically in the next three decades so that by the time the doors closed on the Copley Square Museum for the last time, the collection contained over 420 paintings – nearly 300 of which were acquired since 1890! Although the Museum did make astute purchases – to enhance the collection, or to fill in areas not collected in Boston locally – by far the largest number of paintings came to the Museum each year as gifts – both large and small – from generous and public-spirited local collectors. They were gifts from Boston to Boston, which, during these early years on Copley Square gave the Museum an extraordinarily rich base upon which to grow.

PAMELA S. TABBAA

Fig. 1
Construction of the Museum of Fine Arts on
Huntington Avenue, Spring 1908.

Fig. 2
Museum of Fine Arts, Boston. Bird's-eye view
of completed buildings (Guy Lowell, architect).

The Evans Wing

On April 11, 1907, ground was broken for the Museum of Fine Arts's new building on Huntington Avenue, on a site less than a mile west of its original Copley Square location. Two and a half years later, on November 9, 1909, the grand Beaux-Arts building designed by Boston architect Guy Lowell opened its doors, and the Museum joined a group of other Boston institutions – the Massachusetts Historical Society (1899); the Boston Symphony Orchestra (1900); Horticultural Hall (1901); the New England Conservatory of Music (1902); the Isabella Stewart Gardner Museum (1903); and Harvard Medical School (1906) – whose newly erected buildings were fast making the Fenway area a new cultural and educational center in Boston. In Lowell's Museum building, the wing to the east of the grand central staircase was occupied by impressive collections of Egyptian and Classical art, while the celebrated Asian collection, then as now, was housed in the galleries to the west. The paintings – modern American, French, and English pictures, old masters, and so-called primitives – numbering over 400 works, were displayed temporarily in a succession of rooms running east to west flanking a great rotunda along the Fenway side of the Museum, while a donor was sought to finance a grand paintings wing planned for the northern half of the Huntington Avenue lot.

The Museum did not have long to wait. In May of 1911, Maria Antoinette Evans, widow of self-made mining and rubber magnate Robert Dawson Evans, offered to underwrite the construction of the paintings wing in memory of her husband. Her gift, which eventually amounted to one million dollars, made the MFA the first major American museum to have an endowed wing dedicated exclusively to pictures. The Evans Wing housed twelve paintings galleries, a marble hall for tapestries, print rooms, curatorial offices, a lecture hall, and storerooms for paintings and works on paper.

At Mrs. Evans's death in 1917, the Museum also received a generous purchase fund and a collection of some fifty pictures. The Evanses favored old-master paintings, especially Dutch and Flemish, and, although time has devalued a few of these works' attributions, their Jordaens (*Man and His Wife*; no. 8) and Bol remain among the most highly regarded Northern Baroque paintings in the Museum's collection. They also owned a few early Italian pictures and some strong eighteenth-century French paintings (including the lively Vigée-Lebrun *Portrait of a Young Woman*; no. 25). Sharing with contemporary collectors Henry Clay Frick, J. P. Morgan, and Collis P. Huntington an enthusiasm for aristocratic British portraiture, they acquired three works by Reynolds and three by Lawrence, as well as portraits by Raeburn, Romney, Hoppner, and Gainsborough. More characteristic of local taste was their interest in recent French paintings, which to many Bostonians meant the Barbizon School. Their 1917 bequest to the Museum of Fine Arts included works by Corot, Millet, Daubigny, and Rousseau.

Accompanying the opening of the Evans Wing in February of 1915 was a special loan exhibition of 110 paintings, drawn from the collections of some thirty-five Bostonians. The biggest lenders were Mrs. Evans and Mrs. Henry C. Angell, whose collection of paintings, predominantly nineteenth-century French, would come to the Museum in 1919. That exhibition, with its emphasis on "classical masters" (mainly Italian Baroque and British painting) and on modern French art, provided both an echo of the Museum's permanent collection, formed in the Copley Square years, and a preview of the collection's future direction. Barbizon masters were most generously represented (seven Corots, six Daubignys, and four Millets, among others), but there were also a few more modern French paintings (including a Monet, two Renoirs, a Pissarro, and Manet's *Street Singer* [no. 37]), which anticipated the tremendous influx of Impressionist paintings in the following decade.

The American section of the Evans Wing opening loan exhibition was also representative of the Museum's past, but it provided less of an inkling of its future. The display was divided into two categories: Early American (Copley, Stuart, and Allston) and Later American (painters active from about 1860 forward, with special emphasis on local favorites such as William Morris Hunt, Winslow Homer, John Singer Sargent, and Museum School professor Frank Benson). The early and mid-nineteenth-century genre and landscape paintings that would become the crown jewels of the

Fig. 3
Frances Emily Hunt, *Museum of Fine Arts, Evans Memorial Wing*, 1917, oil on canvas (Gift of Vose Galleries of Boston, Inc., 1981).

Fig. 4
Installation of an old master gallery in the Evans Wing, ca. 1930, showing, among others, nos. 5, 9, 10, and 11.

Fig. 5
Music room, Robert Dawson Evans House, 17
Gloucester Street, Boston, ca. 1910, showing two
portraits by Sir Joshua Reynolds and, reflected in
the mirror, Vigée-Le Brun's *Portrait of a Young
Woman* (no. 25).

Museum's celebrated American art collection did not yet exist for Bostonians. Nevertheless, with the opening of the Evans Wing and the concurrent exhibition of works borrowed from local benefactors who could reasonably be expected to continue to contribute to the growth of the collection, the Museum was making an important statement. Heretofore esteemed as the greatest repository of ancient and oriental art in America, the Museum of Fine Arts proclaimed its intention of becoming preeminent in the collecting of paintings as well.

The Triumph of Impressionism

Visitors to the Museum of Fine Arts today enjoy one of the richest and most comprehensive collections of Impressionist paintings in the United States. They can trace the history of Monet's career from the earliest, Barbizon-influenced works of the 1860s to the water lily pictures of the twentieth century, and view multiple examples of the many series – the haystacks, Rouen cathedral, water lilies – for which he is famous. They can see eighteen Renoirs – not only the popular figurative subjects but also an exquisite early still life and such outdoor scenes as *Landscape on the Coast, near Menton* (no. 51), which were so much admired by the artist's first local patrons. The collection also includes fifteen paintings by Degas, eight by Manet, and five Pissarros, as well as numerous works by lesser masters and, among the Post-Impressionists, a remarkable group of van Goghs and Cézannes and Gauguin's masterpiece *D'où venons-nous? (Where do we come from?*; no. 58). Although a handful of these paintings were purchased by the Museum, the large majority came through the generosity of Boston collectors, who began buying Impressionist works in quantity in the 1880s and '90s – not long after these painters first won public acceptance in France – and made their gifts to the Museum in the three decades following the opening of the Evans Wing.

Boston's first and greatest enthusiasm has always been for the landscapes of Claude Monet. Monet's earliest supporters in Boston began collecting his works during the

1890s, and belonged to the generation following that which had patronized Jean-François Millet. There was little overlapping of the two groups. No late nineteenth-century collector sold off his Millets and other Barbizon paintings to make room for the Impressionists, and, with the exception of Henry Angell, Peter Chardon Brooks, and Denman Waldo Ross (whose 1906 gifts of three Monets [see no. 56] were the first by the artist to enter the Museum's collection), no connoisseur avidly pursued both styles. The patrons of Millet and other Barbizon painters nonetheless expressed admiration for the new art (Quincy Adams Shaw reportedly commented, "The only way to have them is about a mile off – then they are superb.") and, in championing an artist whose radical style placed him far outside the academic mainstream, Boston's fervor for Monet was a natural outgrowth of its admiration for Millet.

Also like Millet, whose works were introduced in Boston by his fellow painter and disciple William Morris Hunt, Monet came to be known here through the efforts of local painters who worked beside him at Giverny. In 1889 Lilla Cabot Perry brought one of the first works by Monet to arrive in the city; she would subsequently lecture on his paintings, introduce Boston patrons to him in France, and in 1927 publish her reminiscences of the painter. An additional imprimatur was provided by the locally popular artists John Singer Sargent and the young Dennis Miller Bunker, both of whom painted with Monet at Giverny.

It was hardly necessary for the late nineteenth-century Bostonian to travel to France to buy Monets, for works by the painter were for sale in Boston from the 1880s. In 1883, the Foreign Exhibition held in Boston included three Monets, all lent by the artist's dealer Durand-Ruel. In 1892, the first exhibition devoted exclusively to the artist's work was held at the St. Botolph Club; Boston collectors lent twenty paintings, or half the number known to be locally owned, according to the catalogue. And in 1913, the pioneering collector Desmond Fitzgerald, who had been lending Monets to the MFA since the 1880s, opened a gallery adjacent to his Brookline home to display a collection of Impressionist paintings that included nine Monets. By the time the Evans Wing opened in 1915, the Museum had been given four Monets, three of which had been in the St. Botolph Club show. Over the next twelve years, eighteen more were donated (including four in 1919 as a result of the gifts of the Alexander Cochrane and John Pickering Lyman collections, which also brought the MFA its first paintings by Renoir and Sisley). In 1927 the Museum honored its favorite Impressionist painter with a large memorial exhibition, which included its twenty-two Monets and an impressive number of local loans.

Several other Impressionist paintings entered Boston collections at an early date, some as a result of friendship with locally popular artists. The first Pissarro to be owned by a Bostonian was purchased about 1875 by Henry Angell at the suggestion of local painter J. Foxcroft Cole. It was Mary Cassatt who urged the acquisition of the city's first two Manets, the *Street Singer* (bought about 1905 by Sarah Choate Sears; no. 37) and the *Execution of Emperor Maximilian* (purchased by Frank Gair Macomber in 1909; no. 36). Both Pissarro and Manet, as well as Renoir, Sisley, and Boudin, all of whom had been shown in the 1883 Foreign Exhibition, were well rrepresented in the MFA collection by the 1920s. In no other American museum, with the possible exceptions of the Metropolitan Museum of Art and the Art Institute of Chicago, could so many important Impressionist pictures be seen so soon after their execution.

The Museum only occasionally bought Impressionist and Post-Impressionist pictures in the 1920s and '30s; nonetheless, these few purchases showed remarkable foresight. Monet's *Rouen Cathedral at Dawn* was acquired in 1924, to be complemented, fifteen years later, by the gift of *Rouen Cathedral in Full Sunlight* (nos. 48 and 49); Degas's *Carriage at the Races* (no. 39) was bought in 1926, and in 1936 the Museum purchased its great Gauguin (no. 58), a painting hailed as the artist's masterpiece and cited by the press as "one of the most exciting events in the history of the Museum of Fine Arts." In subsequent decades, important works by Caillebotte, Cézanne, and Monet (including the ever-popular *La Japonaise*) were purchased by the Museum. For the most part, however, the Museum's collection of Impressionist paintings grew through gifts. They came not, as its Millet collection had, mainly

Fig. 6
Robert Treat Paine, 2nd (1861-1943).

through the generosity of a single donor (Quincy Adams Shaw), but from dozens of Bostonians – among them Anna Perkins Rogers, Mrs. Walter Scott Fitz, Arthur Tracy Cabot, and David P. Kimball. From this distinguished group, three outstanding collectors emerge: the Edwards family, Robert Treat Paine, 2nd, and John Taylor Spaulding.

Juliana Cheney Edwards Collection

The largest single gift of Impressionist paintings came to the Museum in 1939 as part of the Juliana Cheney Edwards Collection, presented as the bequest of Robert, Hannah, and Grace Edwards in memory of their mother. The collection was assembled between about 1907 and 1924, the year of Robert's death; it featured ten paintings by Monet (by far the most works by the artist given by a single donor), six Renoirs, three Pissarros, and works by Sisley, Boudin, and Degas – 57 paintings and watercolors in all. The rest of the paintings given by the Edwardses represented a number of national schools; their taste in old masters paralleled that of the Evanses, with whom they were roughly contemporary. There were several formal British portraits (including the fine Gainsboroughs of Captain and Mrs. Thomas Matthew), a few earlier French pictures, and a small group of American paintings (among them a Copley, a Stuart, a Sully, a regal Sargent portrait, and nine watercolors by the American Impressionist – and local favorite – Dodge MacKnight).

The Edwards bequest (part of which had been shown in a small exhibition in 1927) was announced with an exhibition of the entire collection in December of 1939, following the death of the last surviving sister, Grace. Newspaper accounts of the disposition of her estate revealed her to be not only a collector of great discernment but also typically Bostonian in her generosity to local institutions, particularly those dedicated to public service. With the bulk of her fortune she established a fund for the education of deserving young people in the city of Boston and provided a million-dollar grant to Massachusetts General Hospital. The remainder was divided among cultural and educational institutions along the Fenway: the YMCA, Northeastern University, the Boston Symphony Orchestra, and the

MFA. In addition to the Edwards paintings, the Museum received a substantial purchase fund that later made possible the acquisition of some of its finest pictures.

Robert Treat Paine, 2nd

Robert Treat Paine, 2nd, was born in 1861, the only child of William Cushing Paine and Hannah Hathaway Perry, and nephew and namesake of the dynamic Robert Treat Paine. The family fortune came from railroad and mining property and was augmented by profitable investments by the elder Robert Treat Paine, who retired early and dedicated himself to charitable and philanthropic work. Whereas the senior Paine's interests were primarily in education and social reform – he endowed a fellowship at Harvard for social and ethical studies, began the better housing movement in Boston, and directed the Boston Children's Aid Society – he nonetheless left an important artistic legacy. He was the leading force on the building committee of Trinity Church, a long-term patron of H. H. Richardson, and a collector of nineteenth-century European furniture. His grandson, Robert Treat Paine, Jr., was a brilliant collector of Japanese prints and served for over thirty years as a curator in the Museum's Department of Asiatic Art. And his nephew, Robert Treat Paine, 2nd, a Harvard-trained lawyer and businessman by profession, was the greatest connoisseur in the Paine family dynasty, acquiring superb works in areas as diverse as medieval tapestries, old master drawings, and post-Impressionist paintings.

Unlike the Edwardses, who collected in quantity and presented the Museum with the whole of their efforts, Paine sought masterpieces individually chosen. His gifts evince wide interests and remarkably high standards. Beginning in 1926, and continuing for eighteen years until his death, Paine gave the Museum the best examples from his large collection: paintings by Tintoretto and Fragonard, a rare fifteenth-century Franco-Flemish tapestry from Knole, three Boucher drawings, several pieces of Sèvres porcelain, and three extraordinary nineteenth-century French portraits: Degas's revealing marriage portrait of his sister and their cousin, *Edmondo and Thérèse Morbilli* (no. 41), Cézanne's picture of his wife seated in a red armchair in their apartment in the Montparnasse section of Paris (no.

43), and van Gogh's striking *Postman Joseph Roulin* (no. 42). To this group was added Manet's *Victorine Meurend* (no. 40), presented in Paine's memory in 1946 by his son, Richard Cushing Paine. These four great iconic portraits contrasted markedly with prevailing Boston taste for Impressionist landscape, and filled major gaps in the Museum's collection. Never honored in a special exhibition, Paine's gifts came singly and were, by and large, unheralded – simply taking their places in the galleries, where the strength and quality of each work made it a riveting presence on the wall.

John Taylor Spaulding

Boston collectors have been known for the diversity of their interests: Quincy Adams Shaw collected Renaissance sculpture and pictures by Millet; Robert Treat Paine, 2nd, displayed Rembrandt, Matisse, Seurat, and Copley; Dr. Denman Waldo Ross bestowed gifts on every curatorial department in the Museum. But perhaps no Boston patron of the arts was more eclectic than John Taylor Spaulding, who first put together an unrivaled collection of Japanese prints and then assembled the most comprehensive group of Impressionist and Post-Impressionist paintings to come to the MFA.

The son of the founder of the Revere Sugar Refinery, John Taylor Spaulding, like his older brother William, was Boston born, Harvard educated, and well traveled. In 1909, the two brothers journeyed to Japan and began buying *ukiyo-e* prints. Their collection of over 6,000 prints of the highest quality and superb state of preservation was formed in about a decade, with purchases in Japan arranged by the brothers' agent, architect Frank Lloyd Wright. The Spauldings presented these works to the Museum in 1921, and they are now acknowledged as among the preeminent examples of such prints in the world.

By the time of the brothers' gift of the Japanese prints, John Spaulding was already building another collection. Again an artist was his guide and agent – this time, Charles Hovey Pepper, a local painter, the chairman of the Art Committee of the Boston Art Club, and a childhood friend of Spaulding's. At Pepper's urging, Spaulding joined the club and became acquainted with many artist-members. He soon began buying

their works, as well as those by modern French painters also exhibiting at the club.

Already by 1925, Spaulding's collection of modern painting was well known and much admired. Profiling the collection in *Arts* magazine that year, critic Forbes Watson praised the breadth of the collector's interests, noting perceptively that, unlike many admirers of oriental art, Spaulding did not become "intoxicated and hypnotized by a kind of aesthetic incense" to the point where all Western art came to seem "crude and rough and brazen;" rather, his interest in modern art – first American, then French – followed his involvement with Japanese, and his second collection was formed with the same concerns for condition and quality.

Spaulding's paintings collection, formed in the '20s and first shown at the MFA in 1931, contained works by almost all the major avant-garde French artists of the nineteenth and twentieth centuries, from Courbet, Daumier, and Fantin-Latour to Cézanne, Bonnard, and Matisse. However, unlike the *ukiyo-e* collection, which Spaulding assembled to provide a representative and historic survey of the subject, the paintings were bought according to his own tastes and inclinations – although he kept an eye on the Museum's collection, filling its gaps and avoiding the areas of its greatest strengths. Thus, Spaulding owned three paintings by Degas, but only one Monet (no. 52); while the Museum would own thirty-four Monets by the time of his gift of the collection in 1948, his would be the only work from the 1860s. Spaulding's were the first Cézannes and van Goghs (see nos. 54 and 55) to enter the Museum's collection after those of Robert Treat Paine, 2nd; his was the first Toulouse-Lautrec oil, and his three Gauguins the first to come to the Museum after the *D'où venons-nous*. Spaulding also bought a large group of paintings by a number of American artists active in the 1920s and '30s; his 1948 bequest provided the Museum with its finest – and often its only – examples of works by Bellows, Kent, Henri, and Hopper (the superb *Drug Store*, as well as nine watercolors). Spaulding especially admired still lifes, and ultimately owned twenty by artists as diverse as Fantin-Latour (no. 50), Gauguin, Prendergast, and Macdonald-Wright. To complement this aspect of his collection, Spaulding bought an elegant still

Fig. 7
John Taylor Spaulding (1870-1948).

life by Chardin, *Bronze Goblet and Fruit*; this, too, came to the Museum in 1948.

The Spaulding gift of ninety paintings and pastels, of which half were French, marked the climax – though hardly the conclusion – of Boston's thirty-year enthusiasm for French Impressionist painting. Benefactors like the Edwardses, Paine, and Spaulding had made the Museum preeminent in this area, and, between the opening of the Evans Wing and Spaulding's gift, the collection grew by some seventy Impressionist works.

1948 was a banner year for the Museum of Fine Arts, for it brought not only the Spaulding bequest but also the second half of the M. and M. Karolik Collection of American Paintings. With this single gift of some 233 nineteenth-century paintings, the Museum's holdings evolved from a small and parochial representation of American art into the most important collection in the country. At the same time, Karolik's gift was the culmination of the Museum's efforts to increase its representation of American art, for, since the opening of the Evans Wing, the curators – through purchase and gifts from many Boston donors – had steadily built up an unrivaled collection of works by artists who were the predecessors of the figures Karolik had championed: the colonial portrait painters. And as the decades following the opening of the Evans Wing had seen the ascendancy of Impressionist painting in Boston, so that same period saw the development of the paintings collection's other great strength: American art.

The Emergence of American Painting

Colonial Portraiture

The now-famed collection of American colonial portraiture in the Museum of Fine Arts grew slowly in the Copley Square years. Although some of these portraits, remaining in the families of the original sitters, were loaned for various occasions (notably the Gilbert Stuart exhibition of

1880), the Museum owned, after thirty-five years of collecting, only five paintings by Copley, four by Stuart, two Smiberts, one West, and three portraits by Trumbull. The first portraits to become part of the permanent collection were of public figures, especially those tied to the political history of Boston: in 1876, the sitter's daughter gave the Museum Gilbert Stuart's portrait of Josiah Quincy, the city's mayor in the 1820s and subsequently president of Harvard. Copley's *Watson and the Shark* (no. 20) was an 1889 gift, followed in 1895 by the artist's portrait of Dr. Joseph Warren, the revolutionary hero killed at the Battle of Bunker Hill. Trumbull's portrait of Alexander Hamilton came in 1894. These paintings joined a distinguished group of portraits of political leaders placed on deposit at the Museum in 1876 by the City of Boston and the Boston Athenaeum: Copley's *John Hancock* and *Samuel Adams* (no. 19), as well as Stuart's *George Washington* and *Martha Washington* (the "Athenaeum portraits"), his stirring *Washington at Dorchester Heights*, and *General Henry Knox* (no. 18), a hero at that same battle.

The pace of acquisitions quickened after the opening of the Evans Wing. In the decade of the 1910s, thirteen works by colonial masters were donated, and in the 1920s, when interest in American art of the Revolutionary period began to blossom nationwide, the Museum was a great beneficiary, receiving a Badger, three Blackburns, eleven Copleys (including the rare early double portrait of *Mary and Elizabeth Royall* and several history paintings from his English career), thirteen Stuarts, Trumbull's early *Self-Portrait*, and several others. In the 1930s, twenty-four paintings by colonial masters were acquired, led by Copley's *Paul Revere* (no. 65), and in the 1940s, the Museum added seventeen portraits. The numbers have grown steadily with each decade, and even in the last few years the Museum has acquired, through purchase and gift, twenty eighteenth-century American paintings, many of which had long been on loan, including Copley's poignant *Boy with a Squirrel* (no. 66) and Greenwood's historic *Greenwood-Lee Family* (no. 60), complementing the other great family portraits by Smibert, Blackburn, Copley, and West (see nos. 59, 61, and 62) already in the collection.

Fig. 8
Gilbert Stuart, *Washington at Dorchester Heights*,
1806, oil on panel (Deposited by the City of
Boston, 1876).

Unlike the Museum's Impressionist holdings, the majority of these works came not from a handful of collectors but rather from many different individuals, most of them Bostonians and the descendants of the sitters. Why was there a dramatic increase in interest in colonial portraiture in the 1920s, and a sudden outpouring of generosity toward the Museum of Fine Arts? Quite simply because for the first time colonial portraits were seen not just as treasured family heirlooms or local artifacts but as art worthy of display in a museum.

Boston's enthusiasm for colonial portraiture, beginning in the 1920s, was part of a national trend, inspired at least in part by patriotic feelings after the first World War. In a desire to turn away from Europe and foreign influences, American history was studied with renewed fervor by such pioneer scholars as Charles Beard and Frederick Jackson Turner, early American literature was revived and reexamined, and colonial and federal styles were emulated in domestic architecture. And the decorative arts of the late eighteenth and early nineteenth century were given increased attention: in 1922, the magazine *Antiques* was founded in order to encourage serious scholarship and collecting of early American art. The same year, the Metropolitan Museum of Art mounted an exhibition dedicated to the furniture of Duncan Phyfe, the first American craftsman to be so honored. The exhibition was a prelude to the opening in 1924 of the Metropolitan Museum's American Wing, containing period rooms featuring American furniture, silver, ceramics, and paintings from the late seventeenth century to 1825. That wing was the first large-scale, permanent installation of this material to appear in a major museum. ("American Art really exists!" proclaimed one headline.) Five years later, the Girl Scout loan exhibition, held in New York, confirmed the migration of early American arts from musty parlors and historical societies to museums and art galleries. Though primarily a display of decorative arts, the exhibition contained paintings by Copley, Stuart, Charles Willson Peale, and other colonial masters.

The Museum of Fine Arts was not idle during these years. In the 1920s and '30s, several shows of early American art were mounted, with special attention paid to local craftsmen. A large Gilbert Stuart com- memorative, organized on the occasion of the one hundredth anniversary of the artist's death, was held in 1928. In 1930, the Museum hosted an exhibition in honor of the tercentenary of Massachusetts Bay Colony, "A Loan Exhibition of One Hundred Colonial Paintings," including sixteen pictures from local lenders, who eventually gave them to the Museum. In 1938, the two hundredth anniversary of the birth of John Singleton Copley was celebrated in a special exhibition and accompanied by the first extensive scholarly monograph on the artist. The book, by Barbara N. Parker and Anne B. Wheeler, was the culmination of a series of studies of colonial masters produced in this period – Blackburn in 1923, Stuart in 1926, and Feke in 1930.

Leading the revival of interest in early American art was a group of collectors whose energy and buying power attracted a great deal of attention in the 1920s. Henry Francis DuPont, Henry Ford, and Francis P. Garvan all began collecting during this time; they competed with one another for objects, spent breathtaking sums at auction (DuPont reportedly spent $44,000 for a Philadelphia high chest in 1929), and established museums to further public appreciation of American art of the colonial and federal periods: Henry Ford's Greenfield Village in Dearborn, Michigan, was founded in 1929; in 1930, Garvan gave his collection to Yale; and in the same year, DuPont opened Winterthur, the family home he began remodeling in 1924. Paralleling – and often working with – these collectors were a group of antiquarians and curators (such as Wallace Nutting, Henry Davis Sleeper, John Marshall Phillips at Yale, and R. T. H. Halsey at the Metropolitan Museum) whose efforts in the '20s and '30s advanced both scholarship and public appreciation of American art. In Boston, the dominant forces in this cause were Edwin J. Hipkiss, Keeper of the Department of Western Arts at the Museum of Fine Arts since 1919, and, even more important, the collector Martha Codman Karolik and her husband Maxim.

The Karoliks' Colonial Treasures

Martha Codman, descended from the Codmans, Pickmans, Rogerses, and Amorys, had a strong sense of family history. As a young woman, she began gathering furnishings, paintings, and documents that had belonged to her ancestors, buying back objects from less interested relatives (in this way she gained possession from her brother-in-law of Copley's portraits of her great-great-grandparents, John and Katharine Amory) and tracking down works dispersed from family collections. Although much of what she accumulated was either decorative arts or archival material, she did acquire an impressive group of family portraits of her forebears: those of Mr. and Mrs. John Amory, Jr. by Stuart, Col. and Mrs. Levi Willard by Winthrop Chandler, a portrait of John Codman by Copley after John Johnston, and the majestic Copley portraits mentioned above.

Codman's antiquarian activities were not confined to paintings and furnishings gathered to decorate her Newport mansion. Around 1897, she purchased the Fairbanks House in Dedham, Massachusetts, one of the finest seventeenth-century houses in New England. The gift was motivated, in her words, by "our love of old landmarks, and for the purpose of having it a public benefit to young and old." It was to this sense of social service as well as her dedication to family tradition that Edwin Hipkiss appealed when in 1922 he approached her for help in acquiring for the Museum the Oak Hill Rooms – a parlor, a bedroom, and a dining room from the house built by the noted architect Samuel McIntire in 1801 for the daughter of a Salem merchant, Elias Haskett Derby. An architect by training with special interest in colonial arts, Hipkiss was a strong advocate of re-creating a colonial environment with period furnishings and appropriate decor; he found a willing partner in Martha Codman, who not only contributed funds for purchasing the rooms but also bought many of the furnishings for the Oak Hill settings.

For Codman, the collaboration with Hipkiss was the first step in becoming a collector, and the first time her art-buying activity expanded beyond the assembling of heirlooms for her own enjoyment. The second step was her marriage in 1928. Maxim Karolik was an unorthodox choice: half her age and from a less-privileged social background, he was a Russian *émigré* with a thick accent and a flamboyant, outspoken manner. Endowed with a pleasing tenor voice, he had made a living providing musical entertainment for fashionable dinner parties, but after marrying Martha

Codman, he adopted a new profession – connoisseur and collector of American art. He became first an enthusiastic partner, then the driving spirit behind his wife's antiquarian efforts, encouraging her to extend her collecting beyond family-related projects. Together they acquired (with the advice of Hipkiss and other experts) major works in all areas of colonial American art – silver, metalwork, ceramics, textiles, furniture (including a superb Philadelphia high chest), and paintings – crowning her collection of colonial portraits with Copley's historic image *Mr. and Mrs. Isaac Winslow*, a rare double portrait and the last work painted by Copley before leaving Boston for England in 1774. In 1938, impelled by Martha Codman Karolik's Bostonian sense of public service and Maxim Karolik's populist ideals, they offered their collection to the Museum of Fine Arts. Three years later, this group of 350 eighteenth-century American objects – the M. and M. Karolik Collection – opened in three specially renovated galleries at the Museum, accompanied by an extensive catalogue prepared by Edwin Hipkiss.

In the catalogue, Hipkiss explained the Karolik objects as both art and artifact. Their forms were derived from English models, yet they "bear the stamp of American traits." These traits have not only visual aspects – restraint of line and proportion, simplicity of decoration, and so on – but also a moral component: they were seen to illustrate earlier values and, for the most part, were made by "little known men" who sought to earn their livelihood through "skill and honesty" in accord with the democratic principles of colonial society. These patriotic statements echoed the egalitarian views of Maxim Karolik, who, in his letter to the director, offered the collection "*to the people* through the Museum of Fine Arts." Otherwise, the collection reflected Martha Codman's background far more than his: most of the objects were high style, were made in urban centers, and were produced for aristocratic patrons by celebrated craftsmen. The next Karolik endeavor would be different.

Fig. 9
Georgine Campbell, *Martha Codman* (1858-1948), watercolor on ivory (Bequest of Maxim Karolik, 1964).

Fig. 10
John Singleton Copley, *John Amory*, 1768, and
Katharine Greene Amory, ca. 1763, oil on canvas
(M. and M. Karolik Collection of Eighteenth-
Century American Arts, 1937).

Maxim Karolik and Nineteenth-Century American Painting

The second Karolik Collection, consisting of 233 American paintings made between 1815 and 1865, was also the result of a partnership between the Museum of Fine Arts and Maxim Karolik. This time, however, Karolik approached the Museum's trustees *before* he began collecting, persuasively appealing for the Museum's support for artists working in America during the time between Gilbert Stuart and Winslow Homer – artists totally neglected by collectors, scholars, and museums until then. In December of 1945, Karolik offered to build a collection of works from what he termed "the barren period" for the Museum, seeking the advice of the curators and allowing them to examine and reject any object he proposed. The paintings were to be shown all together in specially prepared galleries for five years, and then were to be rehung with the rest of the collection. A born proselytizer, Karolik also requested that portions of his collection be made available for loan so that people in other cities could discover the riches of this unknown area of American art; thus, in the 1950s and '60s there were numerous traveling exhibitions of the Karolik collection emanating from the Museum of Fine Arts. Martha and Maxim Karolik made their official proposal to the Museum in December of 1945; six years later, in October of 1951, the M. and M. Karolik Collection of American Paintings, 1815 to 1865, opened to the public in ten special galleries constructed in the area previously dedicated to the collection of classical casts. It was accompanied by a scholarly catalogue by John I. H. Baur that was as groundbreaking as the collection itself.

Karolik's goal in building this second collection was to demonstrate the direction of American painting in the first half of the nineteenth century and to examine in particular the development of landscape and genre. He asserted that his selection was guided by aesthetic rather than antiquarian considerations: he was building a collection of Americana to illustrate America's art, not just its history – yet he refused to be seduced by famous names. "We discarded the motto of the fashionable connoisseur: 'Tell me who the painter is and I will tell you whether the painting is good,'"

Karolik was fond of saying. "Our motto was: 'Tell me whether the painting is good and I will not care who the painter is.'" In pursuing the art of this half-century Karolik was rejecting the prevailing notion that in that era creative impulses had been put aside in favor of the business of forging the new republic. His collection of eighty-four identified artists and many more unnamed hands verifies instead the observation of Mrs. Anna Jameson, an 1837 visitor to the United States: "...I was struck by the manner in which the imaginative talent of the people had thrown itself forth in painting; the country seemed to me to swarm with painters" (from *Memoirs and Essays*, London, 1846, p. 162).

Although not all of Karolik's heroes were strangers to Boston – the collection included works by Washington Allston, John Vanderlyn, Samuel F. B. Morse, and other grand manner painters – most were then very little known, neither practitioners of an academically refined high style nor artists who produced most of their work on lucrative commissions for aristocratic patrons. Rather, they were frequently self-trained, and their paintings reflect direct responses to the American landscape and to small-town and rural life. Several of them – Thomas Cole, Asher B. Durand, William Sidney Mount – now dominate American art textbooks; many more, such as Henry F. Darby or Andrew von Wittkamp (nos. 91 and 92) are known primarily, if not entirely, from their inclusion in the Karolik collection.

Karolik entered into his self-appointed task with gusto. Unlike the "supercollectors" of the previous decade, who made their impact by paying big prices and by founding grand museums that featured historical re-creations of earlier eras, Karolik became visible on the art scene through his unique partnership with the Museum of Fine Arts and through the sheer volume of his buying: he bought almost 300 paintings in six years of active collecting. In his first year of the project, 1943, he acquired sixty-eight pictures, spending about $48,000. American art from the "barren period" was far less costly than the high-style colonial art Karolik had purchased during the previous decade: he rarely paid more than $1,000 for a picture, usually much less. But the figures – and Karolik's reputation as a lover of bargains – are somewhat deceptive, for in

Fig. 11
Maxim Karolik (1893-1963) in 1952 (Courtesy, Boston University Photographic Services).

this period, the era of the Second World War, the art market was depressed, and no American master (expect perhaps the perennially popular Winslow Homer) consistently commanded four-figure prices.

Karolik's genius, then, lay as much in his recognition of works of quality in a period then regarded with indifference as in his instinct for a good buy. With the exception of Abby Aldrich Rockefeller and Col. and Mrs. Edgar William Garbisch, who were building their extraordinary collections of folk art at the same time, he had little competition when he began. Initially, his enthusiasm for early nineteenth-century American painting was shared by only a few dealers – Victor Spark and Robert McIntyre in New York, and Charles Childs and the Vose Galleries in Boston – and an even smaller number of curators – John Baur at the Brooklyn Museum, James Thrall Soby and Dorothy Miller at the Museum of Modern Art and, at the Museum of Fine Arts, W. G. Constable, the British-born and trained curator of paintings since 1938 – a belated convert, if ultimately a sympathetic partner, to Karolik's grand project. Yet, despite the small number of champions for this art at the outset, the time was right for the rediscovery of American paintings.

When Karolik conceived his second collection, the political mood of the country was one of isolationism, of turning away from European influences in favor of native achievement. These nationalistic feelings increased when America entered the war. The most popular contemporary art of the period took as its subject the American scene. The key figures – Grant Wood, John Steuart Curry, and Thomas Hart Benton – were realists: they dealt, for the most part, with homey rural themes having a nostalgic appeal, and painted in a linear style with strong local color. Other, more avant-garde painters such as Georgia O'Keeffe and Stuart Davis were also painting the American scene in this period, in styles more realistic than they had employed before. Karolik's landscape and genre painters were the ancestors of these artists of the 1930s and '40s; their popularity made the public more receptive to the art Karolik championed.

Also in the late '30s and '40s were a series of exhibitions that reawakened interest in the humbler side of America's artistic past. The first of these, the Metropolitan Museum's "Life in America" exhibition,

echoed in many ways the American portions of the 1915 Evans Wing loan show in its emphasis on colonial portraiture and late nineteenth-century painting. Nonetheless, it did include a few works by Bingham and Mount, Henry Inman's *Dismissal of School on an October Afternoon* (no. 84, which Karolik subsequently bought), and several Bierstadts, Kensetts, and Eastman Johnsons. By 1943, when the Museum of Modern Art presented the exhibition "Romantic Painting in America," the artists admired by Karolik were far more generously represented. Karolik himself lent four paintings, including Thomas Cole's *Expulsion from the Garden of Eden* and the anonymous *Meditation by the Sea* (nos. 72 and 76). It was at this exhibition that he discovered Martin Johnson Heade.

Karolik's passion for Heade exceeded that for any other artist he championed. Unable to obtain *Thunderstorm over Narragansett Bay* (Amon Carter Museum, Fort Worth), the painting that had so excited him at the "Romantic Painting in America" exhibition, Karolik pursued and in 1945 acquired Heade's second masterpiece, the eerie *Approaching Storm: Beach near Newport* (no. 77). Thereafter, he sought out Heades from every phase of the artist's career, from early portraits to marsh scenes painted all along the east coast to exotic, South American landscapes and late, sensual still lifes. He eventually acquired about fifty, of which more than half came to the Museum of Fine Arts as the cornerstone of the Karolik Collection; the MFA is now the greatest repository of Heade's work in the country. Karolik also admired Fitz Hugh Lane, the Gloucester marine painter, collecting especially his majestic harbor views and late, moody seascapes rather than his more conventional ship portraits; and he drew widely from the work of Albert Bierstadt, acquiring both his major finished pictures and the fresh, lively oil sketches the artist made on his trips west (e. g., no. 82). The Museum of Fine Arts now owns seventeen of these sketches, all Karolik gifts.

Unlike the first Karolik Collection, which followed in the tradition of Ford, Rockefeller, and DuPont, the second was truly revolutionary, resurrecting long-forgotten artists of great talent and reconstructing a fundamental chapter in the story of American art. (Karolik continued his crusade on behalf of these artists in his third – and last –

Fig. 12
Thomas Moran, *Cliffs, Green River, Utah,* 1872,
watercolor on paper (Gift of Maxim Karolik,
1960).

collection, of American drawings and
watercolors, presented to the Museum in
1962. This collection, which placed equal
emphasis on academic and folk drawings,
also included Civil War pictures, works by
visiting foreign artists, and sculpture, thus
rounding out the picture of artistic activity
in America in the first half of the nineteenth
century.) Karolik's discoveries – Heade,
Lane, and, among a group of paintings that
came to the Museum after Karolik's death
in 1963, John F. Peto (see no. 94) – caused
history to be rewritten, for these artists were
relatively little known even in their own
time. Now, thanks to his energies, they are
viewed as major figures in nineteenth-century American art. Equally significant were
the artists – especially Bierstadt and other
western painters – rescued by Karolik after
long periods of critical disdain (as recently
as 1931, one critic snidely called Thomas
Moran [represented in the collections by
fifteen brilliant watercolors] "the Bougue-

reau of landscape"). Recognizing the aesthetic merit of folk art and the appropriate-
ness of such material for a museum collection was yet another of Maxim Karolik's
contributions. Before his galleries opened
to the public in 1951, few of the artists he
championed were sought by collectors,
made the subject of exhibitions, or shown
prominently in museum galleries. Today,
Karolik's taste has come to represent what is
most valued in American art: the artists he
favored are still the most sought after. The
Karolik collections are an unparalleled
assertion of pride in national cultural
achievement; they have made the Museum
of Fine Arts the premier place to see American art of the eighteenth and nineteenth
centuries.

Moving toward the Present

The MFA paintings collection has grown enormously from the small group of forty-six works with which it opened its doors in 1876. Each generation has been responsible for bringing not only beloved single images but whole areas of great strength. The founders contributed the core of the old master collection and a celebrated group of Barbizon paintings, especially the work of Jean-François Millet (saluted in an exhibition held here in 1984 and now traveling in Japan). The opening of the Evans Wing in 1915 inspired benefactors to share with the public their more recent enthusiasms for Impressionist and colonial American painting; as a result, the MFA's holdings are unsurpassed in these areas among American museums. And in 1948, the gifts of two equally brilliant (though very different) collectors, John Taylor Spaulding and Maxim Karolik, enriched the representation of early modern French painting and added nineteenth-century American art to its areas of great strength, thus bringing the Museum closer to the founders' goal of creating a world-class paintings collection.

Over the last three decades, important old master paintings have been acquired, including Lucas van Leyden's *Moses and the Israelites after the Miracle of Water from the Rock*, the great Rosso *Dead Christ with Angels*, and works by Salomon van Ruysdael, Domenico Fetti, and other Baroque masters. The Impressionist collection has also continued to grow, by purchase and by gift. Since the Spaulding bequest, benefactors of the Museum have presented works by Manet, Degas, Boudin, and Cassatt (including her striking portrait *Ellen Mary Cassatt in a White Coat*). The Monet collection has burgeoned: in 1961, the MFA was given the superb *Water Garden and Japanese Footbridge, Giverny* (no. 57), and since then, five more of his paintings have been accessioned, including three given in a single year, 1978. The pattern is much the same for American paintings: recent gifts and purchases have secured works that had previously hung here on loan (such as Copley's *The Copley Family* [no. 62] and Greenwood's *Greenwood-Lee Family* [no. 60]), in

addition to nineteenth-century paintings (such as Heade's *Coast of Jamaica* and a delightful folk portrait by Susan Waters, *The Lincoln Children*), that are very much in the Karolik spirit.

A great collection cannot be content simply to build on its strengths and pursue only the kind of works with which it has long been associated. Consequently, new areas of interest have been developed in recent years, and new partnerships formed between curator and collector. In paintings there have been concerted efforts to fill the gaps in the old masters collection, specifically eighteenth-century Italian and seventeenth-and eighteenth-century French, and to balance our abundant holdings of Monet, Degas, and Renoir with works such as Caillebotte's *Fruit Displayed on a Stand* and other superb examples by lesser-known Impressionist masters. Most important, the Museum has been striving to build a significant collection of twentieth-century art, American and European.

To this end, a Department of Contemporary Art was founded in 1971 and in 1975 generous friends, Henry and Lois Foster, provided a gallery dedicated to the display of twentieth-century art. Now located on the first floor of the new West Wing, this gallery is one of the most visible, and most visited, spaces in the Museum. Major works have been eagerly sought: with the acquisition of twenty-six canvases by the Washington artist Morris Louis, the MFA has become the nation's major repository for color-field painting and is now branching out in many different directions. Among the many works acquired is a dramatic Franz Kline (the gift of Susan Morse Hilles), a superb cubist Picasso, and Stuart Davis's masterpiece, *Hot Still-Scape for Six Colors – Seventh Avenue Style*. Individual donors and purchase funds have made other acquisitions possible, including our first major paintings by Wayne Thiebaud, Jim Dine, and a number of other distinguished contemporary masters; with the gift of works by such young painters as Scott Prior, friends of the Museum have furthered the important task of building a collection of paintings by local artists.

As with the Barbizon, the Impressionist, and the American paintings collections, great acquisitions have been complemented by important exhibitions, in which curator and collector have often played mutually supportive roles. In recent years there have been shows dedicated to contemporary artists – Richard Estes (1978), Larry Poons (1981), and Fairfield Porter (1983) – and equally significant for the future of modern art in Boston, to the remarkable holdings of individuals who have been this city's most energetic and foresighted champions of twentieth-century art – notably Graham Gund, William H. Lane, and Lois and Michael Torf – and who represent the latest generation of great Boston collectors.

CAROL TROYEN

The Evans Wing

I
The Legacy
of
the Founders

BARNA DA SIENA
Italian (Sienese), active mid-14th century
1. *The Mystical Marriage of Saint Catherine*, ca. 1350-1360
Tempera on panel, 54⅝ x 43¾ in. (138.9 x 111.0 cm.)
Inscribed above lower register: *Arico di Neri Arighetti fece fare questa
tavola* (modern)
Purchase, Sarah Wyman Whitman Fund, 1915

CARLO CRIVELLI
Italian (Venetian), active 1457-died 1495
2. *The Virgin with the Dead Christ and Saints Mary Magdalen and John*, 1485
Tempera on panel, 34⅞ x 20¾ in. (88.5 x 52.6 cm.)
Signed and dated lower left, on pediment:
OPVS·CAROLI·CRIVELLI·VENETI ·/1·4·8·5
Purchase, James Fund and Anonymous Gift, 1902

ROGIER VAN DER WEYDEN
Flemish, ca. 1400-died 1464
3. *Saint Luke Painting the Virgin*, ca. 1435
Oil and tempera on panel, 53¾ x 43⅛ in. (136.6 x 109.7 cm.)
Gift of Mr. and Mrs. Henry Lee Higginson, 1893

BRAMANTINO (BARTOLOMEO SUARDI)
Italian (Milanese), ca. 1465- died 1530
4. *Virgin and Child*, ca. 1495-1505
Oil and tempera on panel, 18⅛ x 13⅞ in. (45.9 x 35.2 cm.)
Purchase, Picture Fund, 1913

GIOVANNI BATTISTA MORONI
Italian (Venetian), 1520/25-1578
5. *Portrait of a Man and a Boy* (said to be Count Alborghetti and his son),
late 1550s
Oil on canvas, 38⅝ x 32⅞ in. (98.2 x 83.7 cm.)
Purchase, Turner Sargent Fund, 1895

DIEGO RODRIGUEZ DE SILVA Y VELÁZQUEZ
Spanish, 1599-1660
6. *Don Baltasar Carlos with a Dwarf*, 1632
Oil on canvas, 50⅜ x 40⅛ in. (128.1 x 102.0 cm.)
Inscribed center right: AETAT. S ANN[...] / MENS 4
Purchase, Henry Lillie Pierce Fund, 1901

EL GRECO (DOMENICOS THEOTOCOPOULOS)
Greek (worked in Spain), 1541-1614
7. *Fray Hortensio Félix Paravicino*, 1609
Oil on canvas, 44⅛ x 33⅞ in. (112.0 x 86.1 cm.)
Signed center right: *doménikos theotokopoulos / e'poiei*(in
Greek characters)
Purchase, Isaac Sweetser Fund, 1904

JACOB JORDAENS
Flemish, 1593-1678
8. *Man and His Wife*, ca. 1620-1625
Oil on panel, 49 x 36⅜ in. (124.5 x 92.4 cm.)
Robert Dawson Evans Collection.
Bequest of Maria Antoinette Evans, 1917

JAN VAN HUYSUM
Dutch, 1682-1749
9. *Vase of Flowers in a Niche*, ca. 1732-1736
Oil on panel, 35 x 27½ in. (88.9 x 70.0 cm.)
Signed lower right, on marble slab: *Jan van Huysum fecit*
Bequest of Stanton Blake, 1889

REMBRANDT HARMENSZ. VAN RIJN
Dutch, 1606-1669
10. *Portrait of a Man Wearing a Black Hat*, 1634
Oil on panel, 27½ x 20⅞ in. (70.0 x 53.0 cm.)
Signed and dated lower right: *Rembrandt fe / 1634*
Gift of Mrs. Frederick L. Ames in the name of Frederick L. Ames, 1893

REMBRANDT HARMENSZ. VAN RIJN
Dutch, 1606-1669
11. *Portrait of a Woman Wearing a Gold Chain*, 1634
Oil on panel, 27⅜ x 20⅞ in. (69.5 x 53.0 cm.)
Signed and dated upper right: *Rembrandt fe / 1634*
Gift of Mrs. Frederick L. Ames in the name of Frederick L. Ames, 1893

JEAN SIMÉON CHARDIN
French, 1699-1779
12. *Kitchen Table*, 1755 (?)
Oil on canvas, 15⅝ x 18¾ in. (39.8 x 47.5 cm.)
Signed and dated lower right: *Chardin / 17 [55?]*
Gift of Mrs. Peter Chardon Brooks, 1880

JEAN SIMÉON CHARDIN
French, 1699-1779
13. *Still Life with Tea Pot, Grapes, Pears, and Chestnuts*, ca. 1764
Oil on canvas, 12⅝ x 15¾ in. (32.0 x 40.0 cm.)
Signed and dated lower left: *Chardin / 17 [...]*
Gift of Martin Brimmer, 1883

CLAUDE GELLÉE (called LE LORRAIN)
French (worked in Rome), 1600-1682
14. *Apollo and the Muses on Mount Helicon*, ca. 1680
Oil on canvas, 39¼ x 53¾ in. (99.7 x 136.5 cm.)
Signed lower center: PARNASS[...] PARN[...]SS[...] CL[...]D[...]
(indistinct)
Purchase, Picture Fund, 1912

FRANÇOIS BOUCHER
French, 1703-1770
15. *Returning from Market*, 1767
Oil on canvas, 81¼ x 113 in. (206.4 x 287.0 cm.)
Signed and dated lower left, on stone: *F. Boucher / 1767*
Gift of the heirs of Peter Parker, 1871

FRANCESCO GUARDI
Italian (Venetian), 1712-1793
16. *Procession of Gondolas in the Bacino di San Marco*, ca. 1780-1793
Oil on canvas, 38⅝ x 54⅜ in. (98.0 x 138.0 cm.)
Purchase, Picture Fund, 1911

GIOVANNI PAOLO PANNINI
Italian (Roman), 1691-1765
17. *Picture Gallery with Views of Modern Rome,* 1757
Oil on canvas, 67 x 96¼ (170.0 x 244.5 cm.)
Signed lower left, on face of block of stone: I. PAUL PANINI.ROMAE;
dated on edge of stone: *1757*
Purchase, Charles Potter Kling Fund, 1976

GILBERT STUART
American, 1755-1828
18. *General Henry Knox*, ca. 1794-1800
Oil on panel, 47 x 38½ in. (119.4 x 97.8 cm.)
Deposited by the City of Boston, 1876

JOHN SINGLETON COPLEY
American, 1738-1815
19. *Samuel Adams*, ca. 1772
Oil on canvas, 50 x 40¼ in. (127.0 x 102.2 cm.)
Deposited by the City of Boston, 1876

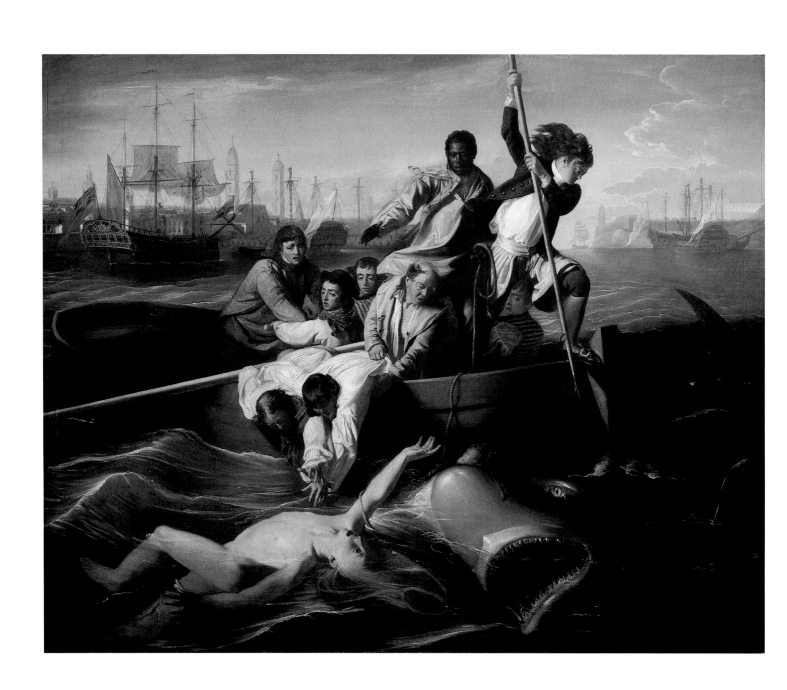

JOHN SINGLETON COPLEY
American, 1738-1815
20. *Watson and the Shark*, 1778
Oil on canvas, 72 x 90¼ in. (182.9 x 229.2 cm.)
Signed and dated inside boat: *J. S. Copley P. 1778*
Gift of Mrs. George von Lengerke Meyer, 1889

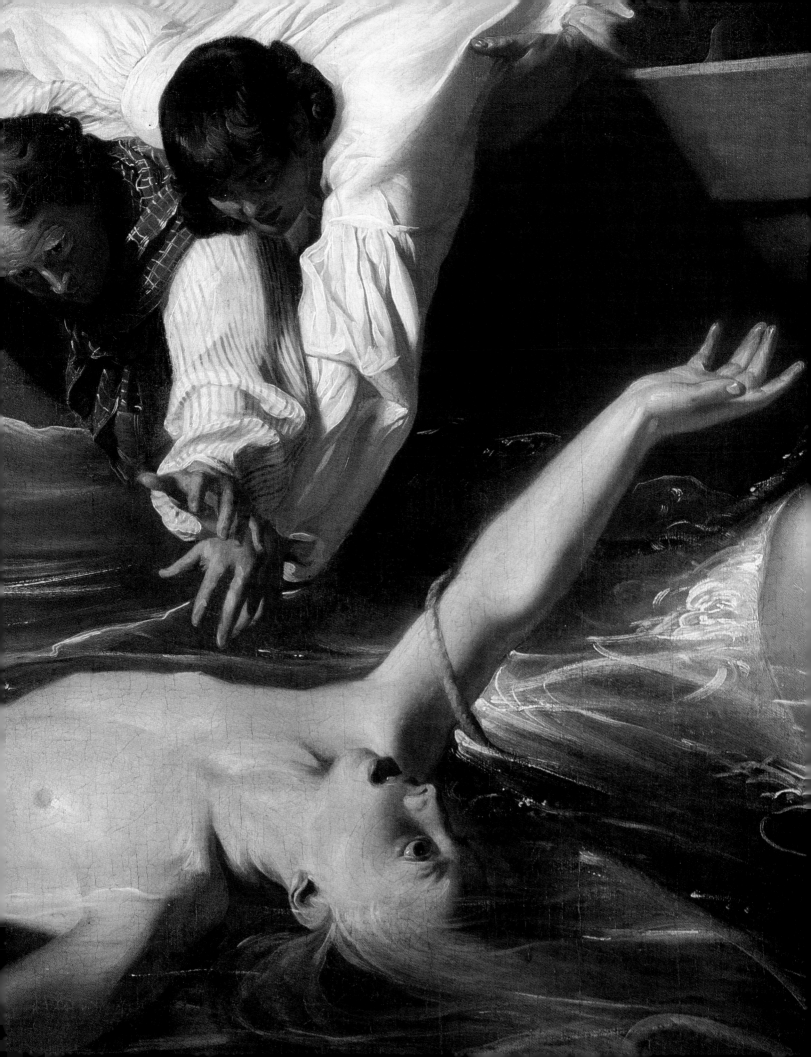

JOHN NEAGLE
American, 1796-1860
21. *Pat Lyon at the Forge*, 1826-1827
Oil on canvas, 93 x 68 in. (236.1 x 172.6 cm.)
Signed and dated lower left: *J. Neagle 1826 & 7--*.
Henry H. and Zoë Oliver Sherman Fund, 1975

THOMAS GAINSBOROUGH
British, 1727-1788
22. *John Eld of Seighford Hall, Stafford*, ca. 1772
Oil on canvas, 94 x 60¼ in. (238.8 x 153.0 cm.)
Inscribed lower right, on base of pedestal: *By the Command / And at the Expence / of the Subscribers*
Purchase, Special Painting Fund, 1912

JEAN BAPTISTE GREUZE
French, 1725-1805
23. *Portrait of a Young Woman (The White Hat)*, ca. 1780
Oil on canvas, 22⅜ x 18¼ in. (56.8 x 46.5 cm.)
**Purchase, Jessie H. Wilkinson, Grant Walker, Seth K. Sweetser,
and Abbott Lawrence Funds, 1976**

JOHN SINGLETON COPLEY
American, 1738-1815
24. *Mrs. Richard Skinner (Dorothy Wendell)*, 1772
Oil on canvas, 39¾ x 30¾ in. (100.9 x 78.1 cm.)
Signed and dated center right: *John Singleton Copley pinx / 1772 / Boston*
Bequest of Mrs. Martin Brimmer, 1906

ELISABETH LOUISE VIGÉE-LE BRUN
French, 1755-1842
25. *Portrait of a Young Woman*, ca. 1797
Oil on canvas, 32⅜ x 27¾ in. (82.2 x 70.5 cm.)
Robert Dawson Evans Collection.
Bequest of Maria Antoinette Evans, 1917

WASHINGTON ALLSTON
American, 1799-1843
26. *Elijah in the Desert*, 1818
Oil on canvas, 48¾ x 72½ in. (123.8 x 184.2 cm.)
Signed and dated on back: *W. Allston 1818*; *W. Allston A. R. A.*
Gift of Mrs. Samuel Hooper and Miss Alice Hooper, 1870

JOSEPH MALLORD WILLIAM TURNER
British, 1775-1851
27. *Slave Ship (Slavers Throwing Overboard the Dead and Dying, Typhon Coming On)*, ca. 1840
Oil on canvas, 35¾ x 48¼ in. (90.8 x 122.6 cm.)
Purchase, Henry Lillie Pierce Fund, 1899

JEAN BAPTISTE CAMILLE COROT
French, 1796-1875
30. *Forest of Fontainebleau*, ca. 1846
Oil on canvas, 35½ x 50¾ in. (90.2 x 128.8 cm.)
Signed lower left: COROT
Gift of Mrs. Samuel Dennis Warren, 1890

JEAN-FRANÇOIS MILLET
French, 1814-1875
31. *Harvesters Resting (Ruth and Boaz)*, 1853
Oil on canvas, 26½ x 47⅛ in. (67.4 x 119.8 cm.)
Signed and dated lower right: *J. F. Millet 1853* (largely effaced in
1970s cleaning)
Bequest of Mrs. Martin Brimmer, 1906

EUGÈNE DELACROIX
French, 1798-1863
32. *Lion Hunt*, 1858
Oil on canvas, 36⅛ x 46¼ in. (91.7 x 117.5 cm.)
Signed and dated lower right: *Eug. Delacroix 1858.*
S. A. Denio Collection. Purchase, Sylvanus Adams Denio Fund, 1895

GUSTAVE COURBET
French, 1819-1877
33. *The Quarry (La Curée)*, ca. 1857
Oil on canvas, 82¾ x 72¼ in. (210.2 x 183.5 cm.)
Signed lower right: *G. Courbet*
Purchase, Henry Lillie Pierce Fund, 1918

WINSLOW HOMER
American, 1836-1910
34. *The Fog Warning*, 1885
Oil on canvas, 30 x 48 in. (76.2 x 121.9 cm.)
Signed and dated lower left: *Winslow Homer 1885*
Otis Norcross Fund, 1894

JOHN SINGER SARGENT
American, 1856-1925
35. *The Daughters of Edward D. Boit*, 1882
Oil on canvas, 87 x 87 in. (221 x 221 cm.)
Signed and dated lower right: *John S. Sargent. 1882.*
Gift of Mary Louisa Boit, Florence D. Boit, Jane Hubbard Boit,
and Julia Overing Boit, in memory of their father, 1919

EDOUARD MANET
French, 1832-1883
36. *Execution of the Emperor Maximilian*, ca. 1867
Oil on canvas, 77⅛ x 102¼ in. (196.0 x 259.8 cm.)
Gift of Mr. and Mrs. Frank Gair Macomber, 1930

EDOUARD MANET
French, 1832-1883
37. *Street Singer*, ca. 1862
Oil on canvas, 67⅜ x 41⅝ in. (171.3 x 105.8 cm.)
Signed lower left: *éd. Manet*
Bequest of Sarah Choate Sears in memory of her husband, Joshua Montgomery Sears, 1966

II
The Triumph
of
Impressionism

EDGAR DEGAS
French, 1834-1917
38. *Race Horses at Longchamp*, ca. 1873-1875
Oil on canvas, 13⅜ x 16½ in. (34.1 x 41.8 cm.)
Signed lower left: *E Degas*
S. A. Denio Collection. Purchase, Sylvanus Adams Denio Fund, 1903

EDGAR DEGAS
French, 1834-1917
39. *Carriage at the Races*, 1872
Oil on canvas, 14⅜ x 22 in. (36.5 x 55.9 cm.)
Signed lower left: *Degas*
Purchase, 1931 Purchase Fund, 1936

EDOUARD MANET
French, 1832-1883
40. *Victorine Meurend*, ca. 1862
Oil on canvas, 16⅞ x 17¼ in. (42.9 x 43.7 cm.)
Signed upper right: *Manet*
Gift of Richard C. Paine in memory of his father, Robert Treat Paine, 2nd, 1946

EDGAR DEGAS
French, 1834-1917
41. *Edmondo and Thérèse Morbilli,* ca. 1867
Oil on canvas, 45⅞ x 34¾ in. (116.5 x 88.3 cm.)
Gift of Robert Treat Paine, 2nd, 1931

VINCENT VAN GOGH
Dutch (worked in France), 1853-1890
42. *The Postman Joseph Roulin*, 1888
Oil on canvas, 32 x 25¾ in. (81.2 x 65.3 cm.)
Gift of Robert Treat Paine, 2nd, 1935

PAUL CÉZANNE
French, 1839-1906
43. *Madame Cézanne in a Red Armchair*, ca. 1877
Oil on canvas, 28½ x 22 in. (72.5 x 56.0 cm.)
Bequest of Robert Treat Paine, 2nd, 1944

PAUL CÉZANNE
French, 1839-1906
44. *Self-Portrait with a Beret*, ca. 1898-1899
Oil on canvas, 25¼ x 21 in. (64.0 x 53.5 cm.)
**Purchase, Charles H. Bayley Picture and Painting Fund and partial gift
of Elizabeth Paine Metcalf, 1972**

CAMILLE PISSARRO
French, 1830-1903
45. *Sunlight on the Road, Pontoise*, 1874
Oil on canvas, 20⅝ x 32⅛ in. (52.3 x 81.5 cm.)
Signed and dated lower right: *C. Pissarro. 1874*
Juliana Cheney Edwards Collection. Bequest of Robert J. Edwards
in memory of his mother, 1925

CLAUDE MONET
French, 1840-1926
46. *Poppy Field in a Hollow near Giverny*, 1885
Oil on canvas, 25⅝ x 32 in. (65.2 x 81.2 cm.)
Signed and dated lower left: *Claude Monet 85*
Juliana Cheney Edwards Collection. Bequest of Robert J. Edwards
in memory of his mother, 1925

CLAUDE MONET
French, 1840-1926
47. *Ravine of the Creuse in Sunlight*, 1889
Oil on canvas, 25⅝ x 36⅜ in. (65.0 x 92.4 cm.)
Signed and dated lower left: *Claude Monet 89*
Juliana Cheney Edwards Collection. Bequest of Robert J. Edwards
in memory of his mother, 1925

CLAUDE MONET
French, 1840-1926
48. *Rouen Cathedral at Dawn*, 1894
Oil on canvas, 41¾ x 29⅛ in. (106.1 x 73.9 cm.)
Signed and dated lower left: *Claude Monet 94*
Tompkins Collection. Purchase, Arthur Gordon Tompkins Fund, 1924

CLAUDE MONET
French, 1840-1926
49. *Rouen Cathedral in Full Sunlight*, 1894
Oil on canvas, 39⅝ x 26 in. (100.5 x 66.2 cm.)
Signed and dated lower left: *Claude Monet 94*
**Juliana Cheney Edwards Collection. Bequest of Hannah Marcy Edwards
in memory of her mother, 1939**

HENRI FANTIN-LATOUR
French, 1836-1904
50. *Flowers and Fruit on a Table*, 1865
Oil on canvas, 23⅝ x 28⅞ in. (60.0 x 73.3 cm.)
Signed and dated lower right: *Fantin - 1865.*
Bequest of John T. Spaulding, 1948

CLAUDE MONET
French, 1840-1926
52. *Rue de la Bavolle, Honfleur*, ca. 1864
Oil on canvas, 22 x 24 in. (55.9 x 61.0 cm.)
Signed lower left: *Claude Monet*
Bequest of John T. Spaulding, 1948

CAMILLE PISSARRO
French, 1830-1903
53. *Pontoise, the Road to Gisors, Winter*, 1873
Oil on canvas, 23½ x 29 in. (59.8 x 73.8 cm.)
Signed and dated lower right: *C. Pissarro 1873*
Bequest of John T. Spaulding, 1948

VINCENT VAN GOGH
Dutch (worked in France), 1853-1890
54. *Houses at Auvers*, 1890
Oil on canvas, 29¾ x 24⅜ in. (75.5 x 61.8 cm.)
Bequest of John T. Spaulding, 1948

VINCENT VAN GOGH
Dutch (worked in France), 1853-1890
55. *Lullaby: Madame Augustine Roulin Rocking a Cradle* (La Berceuse), 1889
Oil on canvas, 36½ x 28⅝ in. (92.7 x 72.8 cm.)
Inscribed lower right, along chair: *La Berceuse*
Bequest of John T. Spaulding, 1948

CLAUDE MONET
French, 1840-1926
56. *Cliffs of the Petites Dalles*, 1880
Oil on canvas, 23⅞ x 31⅝ in. (60.5 x 80.2 cm.)
Signed and dated lower left: *Claude Monet 1880*
Ross Collection. Gift of Denman Ross, 1906

CLAUDE MONET
French, 1840-1926
57. *Monet's Water Garden and Japanese Footbridge, Giverny*, 1900
Oil on canvas, 35⅛ x 36½ in. (89.2 x 92.8 cm.)
Signed and dated lower left: *Claude Monet 1900*
**Given in memory of Governor Alvan T. Fuller by the
Fuller Foundation,** 1961

PAUL GAUGUIN
French, 1848-1903
58. *D'où venons-nous? Que sommes-nous? Où allons-nous? (Where do We
Come from? What are We? Where are We Going?), 1897*
Oil on canvas, 54¾ x 147½ in. (139.1 x 374.6 cm.)
Inscribed upper left: *D'où Venons Nous/ Que Sommes Nous/ Où Allons Nous*
Signed and dated upper right: *P. Gauguin / 1897*
Tompkins Collection. Purchase, Arthur Gordon Tompkins Fund, 1936

JOHN SMIBERT
American, 1688-1751
59. *Daniel, Peter, and Andrew Oliver,* 1732
Oil on canvas, 39¼ x 57¾ in. (99.7 x 144.2 cm.)
Emily L. Ainsley Fund, 1953

JOHN GREENWOOD
American, 1727-1792
60. *The Greenwood-Lee Family*, ca. 1747
Oil on canvas, 55⅝ x 69¼ in. (141.3 x 175.9 cm.)
Bequest of Henry Lee Shattuck in memory of the late Morris Gray, 1983

JOSEPH BLACKBURN
American, active 1752-1778
61. *Isaac Winslow and His Family*, 1755
Oil on canvas, 54½ x 79½ in. (138.4 x 201.9 cm.)
Signed and dated lower left: *I. Blackburn Pinx 1755*
Abraham Shuman Fund, 1942

JOHN SINGLETON COPLEY
American, 1738-1815
62. *The Copley Family*, 1780s
Oil on canvas, 20¾ x 26¼ in. (52.5 x 66.5 cm.)
Henry H. and Zoë Oliver Sherman Fund and Gift of Daniel and Robert Amory,
1977

ROBERT FEKE
American, before 1741-after 1750
63. *Isaac Winslow*, ca. 1748
Oil on canvas, 50 x 40⅛ in. (127.0 x 101.8 cm.)
**Gift in memory of the sitter's granddaughter (Mary Russell Winslow
Bradford, 1793-1899), by her great-grandson, Russell Wiles, 1942**

JOHN SINGLETON COPLEY
American, 1738-1815
64. *Mrs. James Warren (Mercy Otis)*, ca. 1763
Oil on canvas, 51¼ x 41 in. (130.1 x 104.1 cm.)
Bequest of Winslow Warren, 1931

JOHN SINGLETON COPLEY
American, 1738-1815
65. *Paul Revere*, ca. 1768-1770
Oil on canvas, 35 x 28½ in. (88.9 x 72.4 cm.)
Gift of Joseph W., William B., and Edward H. R. Revere, 1930

JOHN SINGLETON COPLEY
American, 1738-1815
66. *Boy with a Squirrel*, 1765
Oil on canvas, 30¼ x 25 in. (76.8 x 63.5 cm.)
Anonymous Gift, 1978

JOHN SINGLETON COPLEY
American, 1738-1815
67. *Mrs. Ezekiel Goldthwait (Elizabeth Lewis)*, 1771
Oil on canvas, 50⅜ x 40¼ in. (128.0 x 102.2 cm.)
Bequest of John T. Bowen in memory of Eliza M. Bowen, 1941

JOHN SINGLETON COPLEY
American, 1738-1815
68. *Ezekiel Goldthwait*, 1771
Oil on canvas, 50⅛ x 40 in. (127.3 x 101.5 cm.)
Signed lower right: JSC (in monogram)
Bequest of John T. Bowen in memory of Eliza M. Bowen, 1941

GILBERT STUART
American, 1755-1828
69. *Anna Powell Mason*, ca. 1807-1810
Oil on wood, 33 x 27⅛ in. (83.8 x 68.9 cm.)
Lucy Dalbiac Luard and Seth K. Sweetser Funds, 1978

GILBERT STUART
American, 1755-1828
70. *Bishop Jean-Louis Anne Magdelaine Lefebvre de Cheverus*, 1823
Oil on canvas, 36¼ x 28⅜ in. (92.1 x 72.1 cm.)
Bequest of Mrs. Charlotte Gore Greenough Hervoches du Quillou, 1921

THOMAS COLE
American, 1801-1848
71. *Sunny Morning on the Hudson River*, ca. 1827
Oil on panel, 18¾ x 25¼ in. (47.6 x 64.1 cm.)
Signed left center: *Cole*
**Gift of Mrs. Maxim Karolik for the Karolik Collection of
American Paintings, 1815-1865, 1947**

THOMAS COLE
American, 1801-1848
72. *Expulsion from the Garden of Eden*, 1828
Oil on canvas, 38¼ x 53¼ in. (97.2 x 135.3 cm.)
Signed lower left: *T. Cole*
**Gift of Mrs. Maxim Karolik for the Karolik Collection of
American Paintings, 1815-1865, 1947**

JASPER F. CROPSEY
American, 1823-1900
73. *Schatacook Mountain, Housatonic Valley, Connecticut*, 1845
Oil on canvas, 30¾ x 46¼ in. (78.1 x 117.4 cm.)
Signed and dated lower left and on rocks: *J. F. Cropsey 1845*;
inscribed on back: *the Valley of the Housatonic, Kent, Conn.*
Gift of Mrs. Maxim Karolik for the Karolik Collection of
American Paintings, 1815-1865, 1947

MARTIN JOHNSON HEADE
American, 1819-1904
75. *Passion Flowers and Hummingbirds*, ca. 1865
Oil on canvas, 15½ x 21½ in. (39.4 x 54.6 cm.)
Signed lower left: *M. J. Heade*
**Gift of Maxim Karolik for the Karolik Collection of
American Paintings, 1815-1865, 1947**

MARTIN JOHNSON HEADE
American, 1819-1904
77. *Approaching Storm: Beach Near Newport*, ca. 1860
Oil on canvas, 28 x 58¼ in. (71.2 x 148.0 cm.)
M. and M. Karolik Collection. Gift of Maxim Karolik, 1945

FITZ HUGH LANE
American, 1804-1865
78. *Castine, Maine*, 1856
Oil on canvas, 21 x 33½ in. (53.3 x 82.5 cm.)
Signed and dated lower right: *F. H. Lane / 1856*
Bequest of Maxim Karolik, 1964

FITZ HUGH LANE
American, 1804-1865
79. *Fresh Water Cove from Dolliver's Neck, Gloucester*, early 1850s
Oil on canvas, 24⅛ x 36 in. (61.3 x 91.5 cm.)
**Bequest of Martha C. Karolik for the Karolik Collection of
American Paintings, 1815-1865, 1948**

FITZ HUGH LANE
American, 1804-1865
80. *Owl's Head, Penobscot Bay, Maine,* 1862
Oil on canvas, 16 x 26 in. (40.6 x 66.0 cm.)
Signed and dated on back: *Owl's Head – Penobscot Bay, by F.H. Lane,* 1862
**Bequest of Martha C. Karolik for the Karolik Collection of
American Paintings, 1815-1865, 1948**

ALBERT BIERSTADT
American, 1830-1902
81. *Wreck of the "Ancon" in Loring Bay, Alaska*, 1889
Oil on paper, mounted on panel, 14 x 19¾ in. (35.6 x 50.2 cm.)
Signed lower right: *A Bierstadt* (A B in monogram)
Gift of Mrs. Maxim Karolik for the Karolik Collection of
American Paintings, 1815-1865, 1947

ALBERT BIERSTADT
American, 1830-1902
83. *The Buffalo Trail*, 1867-1868
Oil on canvas, 32 x 48 in. (81.3 x 122.0 cm.)
Signed lower right: *A Bierstadt* (A B in monogram)
Gift of Mrs. Maxim Karolik for the Karolik Collection of
American Paintings, 1815-1865, 1947

HENRY INMAN
American, 1801-1846
84. *Dismissal of School on an October Afternoon*, 1845
Oil on canvas, 26 x 36 in. (66.0 x 91.4 cm.)
Signed and dated lower left, on rock: *Inman / 1845*
**Bequest of Martha C. Karolik for the Karolik Collection of
American Paintings,** 1815-1865, 1948

THOMAS HICKS
American, 1823-1890
85. *Calculating*, 1844
Oil on canvas, 14 x 16¾ in. (35.5 x 42.5 cm.)
Inscribed on back of canvas before relining: *Calculating / by T. Hicks /*
1844
**Gift of Maxim Karolik to the M. and M. Karolik Collection of
American Paintings, 1815-1865, 1962**

JAMES GOODWYN CLONNEY
American, 1812-1867
86. *In the Cornfield*, 1844
Oil on canvas, 14 x 17 in. (35.5 x 43.2 cm.)
Signed and dated lower left: *J. G. Clonney 1844*
Gift of Mrs. Maxim Karolik for the Karolik Collection of
American Paintings, 1815-1865, 1947

WILLIAM SIDNEY MOUNT
American, 1807-1868
87. *The Bone Player,* 1856
Oil on canvas, 36 x 29 in. (91.4 x 73.6 cm.)
Signed and dated lower right: *Wm. S. Mount 1856*; inscribed on back: *The Bone Player / Painted by Wm S. Mount / 1856*
Bequest of Martha C. Karolik for the Karolik Collection of American Paintings, 1815-1865, 1948

AMERICAN SCHOOL
19th century
88. *Phoebe Drake*, ca. 1815-1825
Oil on canvas, 48¼ x 36 in. (122.6 x 91.4 cm.)
Bequest of Maxim Karolik, 1964

ERASTUS SALISBURY FIELD
American, 1805-1900
89. *The Garden of Eden*, ca. 1860
Oil on canvas, 36¾ x 46 in. (93.4 x 116.8 cm.)
Gift of Maxim Karolik for the M. and M. Karolik Collection of
American Paintings, 1815-1865, 1948

J. D. BUNTING

American, 19th century

90. *View of Darby, Pennsylvania after the Burning of Lord's Mill*, 1840-1850

Oil on canvas, 42 x 51¼ in. (106.7 x 130.8 cm.)

Signed lower right: *J. D. Bunting*

**Gift of Maxim Karolik to the M. and M. Karolik Collection of
American Paintings, 1815-1865, 1962**

HENRY F. DARBY
American, 1829-1897
91. *Reverend John Atwood and His Family*, 1845
Oil on canvas, 72 x 96¼ in. (182.9 x 240.6 cm.)
Signed and dated lower right: *H. F. Darby, Painter / 1845*
**Gift of Maxim Karolik to the M. and M. Karolik Collection of
American Paintings, 1815-1865, 1962**

ANDREW L. VON WITTKAMP
American, 19th century
92. *Black Cat on a Chair*, ca. 1850-1875
Oil on canvas, 36 x 29¼ in. (91.4 x 74.3 cm.)
Signed lower right: *Andrew L. von Wittkamp M.D.*
Bequest of Martha C. Karolik for the Karolik Collection of
American Paintings, 1815-1865, 1948

E. L. GEORGE
American, 19th century
93. *Child in a Rocking Chair*, 1870
Oil on canvas, 15 x 13 in. (38.1 x 33.0 cm.)
Signed and dated lower left: *E. L. George / 1870*
**Gift of Maxim Karolik to the M. and M. Karolik Collection of
American Paintings, 1815-1865, 1962**

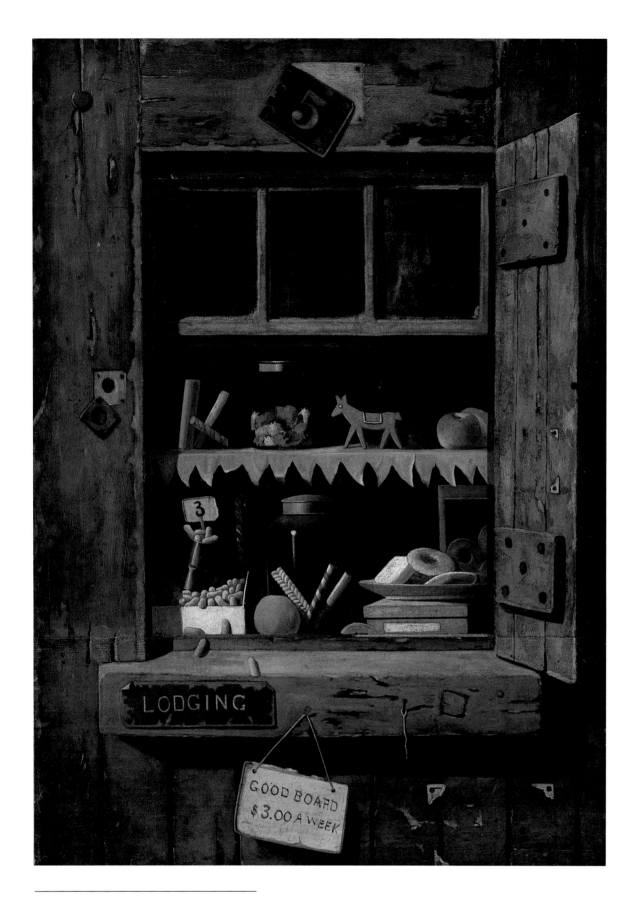

JOHN FREDERICK PETO
American, 1854-1907
94. *The Poor Man's Store*, 1885
Oil on canvas and wood, 36 x 25½ in. (91.4 x 64.8 cm.)
Signed and dated upper left: *J. F. Peto / -85*
Gift of Maxim Karolik to the M. and M. Karolik Collection of
American Paintings, 1815-1865, 1962